Solving Problems

A problem manager's handbook. A guide to implementing problem process for IT services

2/28/2015

Shiva Kumar Bhaskaran

Om Namah Shivaaya!

Acknowledgement

Personal

Thank you God for blessing me with Parents who dedicated their lives to me and without whom, I would not exist!

Thank you to my Wife for encouraging me to write and supporting this effort!

Special thanks to my daughters for allowing me to spend time on this book!

Professional

Thank you Sharada Ma'am (Mrs. Sharada Prasadita), a one-person IT service management university for guiding me through most part of my IT service management learning journey as a mentor rather than a manager!

Thank you Mr. Bharani Kumar, for hand- holding my initial steps in the IT service management learning journey as a friend and supportive manager!

Thank you Mr. Shreeshan Rangayan and Mr. Tejiner Singh Virdi, for giving me the break to begin the IT service management learning journey!

Thank you Mr. Kiran Kumar Pabathi for being a supportive colleague and for being an inspiration to write this book!

About the Author

 Mr. Shiva Kumar Bhaskaran carries about 12 years' experience in IT and ITeS industries. He has worked for industry leaders like IBM, HSBC and Wipro. He is currently employed as a senior process Consultant with one of the leading Indian IT service providers.

Shiva has worked in the IT service management area and in specific problem management for over six years both as a problem manager and process consultant with many implementations along the way across industry verticals like Manufacturing, BFSI, Energy, Utilities, Retail and ITeS, and also across geographies of US, UK, Europe, APAC and India.

Shiva has developed and delivered niche trainings in the areas of capacity (capacity management for capacity managers) and problem (problem management for problem managers). He has also delivered ITIL® Foundation class room trainings in India and US, and also Webinars on other IT service management topics.

By education, Shiva is a Graduate in Computer Science and Mathematics from Osmania University, India. His professional certifications include ITIL® expert, certified lead auditor for ITSM and ISMS quality management systems, COBIT foundation, certified network security manager (CNSM) and Six Sigma black belt. He is also PMP and CCNA trained.

ITIL® is a Registered Trade Mark of AXELOS Limited

Preface

When I started my problem management journey over 6 years ago, I was lucky to have had a few good people around me to guide. As I went about my activities for a few years and then moved onto a Consultant's role guiding, mentoring and supporting problem managers from various accounts (organizations) there is a lot that I got to learn particularly in the areas of proactive and preventive problem identification and problem reporting. There were certainly times when I felt, "I wish I had known this earlier when I started off as a problem manager, I would have been a much better problem manager and also the value to customer/ business from the problem process would have been significantly higher/ superior".

This book is a reflection of my learning of problem management activities over the years and a sincere effort to equip aspiring problem managers with all the knowledge that can, not only decrease their learning curve but also help them become effective in their role from the onset. I envision this book to help all problem managers who are already playing the role and the one's aspiring, drive the process more effectively to deliver faster and superior results.

I invite your honest feedback — siv_santh@yahoo.com

Contents

I.   Setting the context

Mr. Iyer is rushing to catch a rick, the poor cousin of Taxi in India, at 7: 30 AM walking as fast as he can while being careful not to run for the fear of being chased by a canine. He is racing to get to a rick to catch a bus waiting 3.5 KM away which will transport him to his Office 30 KM away. As a regular, he knows that he has 15 minutes before the bus leaves, that it takes the rick 12 minutes to reach the bus boarding point which means he has 3 minutes to- a) cover a distance on foot that takes him 6 minutes to walk, b) and find a rick which usually takes 3- 5 min to find. This is a race! 3 minutes to complete two tasks that normally takes him about 8 minutes!

Mr. Iyer races to reach the rick-point in 4 minutes and with a cheer gets into a waiting rick patting self in the mind. Saying prayers through the 12 minute ride so as not to miss the bus, reaches the bus boarding point a full 60 seconds late but thank God! Today is his day, the bus is just about to leave and relieved, he gets into the bus to relax over the next hour! Content with his performance this morning, after all he made it to the bus exerting himself and completing something that takes 23 minutes in just 16 minutes of course with a little bit of luck, he slips into a power nap while cautioning himself to set the daily wake up alarm promptly on his mobile to avoid this situation in future.

This is not the first time that Mr. Iyer finds himself in this situation going through the anxiety, the exertion, the prayers, the relief and finally the proud contentment with an afterword of caution! It's always the alarm that was not audible or the rick that was too slow or the intimidating canines or the father or wife who failed to wake him up on time (irrespective of the alarm set). Smart Mr. Iyer finds a different reason for each occurrence of the above incident and goes through the motions, at least once a week. The problem is never acknowledged; forget about finding the root cause. Ideally, Mr. Iyer should have figured out by now that he needs to plan better and stick to the plan of early bed time to be able to hear the alarm set and wake up with adequate (buffer) time to make it to the bus without troubling the almighty for help early in the morning.

In the realm of IT service management while the daily heroics of the technical Subject Matter Experts (SME), resolving IT incidents small or big are appreciated and necessary but not sufficient. It is important to develop different kind of heroics, heroics to understand the underlying causes, faults or errors in the IT infrastructure, application and other components like processes, people skills, technology etc., which support delivery of IT services so that we are able to avoid the occurrence or at least, the recurrence of incidents which not only disrupt business and/ or exert very many technical resources but also have the potential of causing far reaching consequences like loss of reputation, loss of customer confidence, loss of revenue etc.,

An example from my problem management experience

After a decent stint as a problem manager, during one of my first assignments as a consultant implementing problem process for a leading UK Utilities Company, I found from the data of incidents triggered by monitoring tool alerts that about 40% of such alert- triggered incidents for Wintel technology were from a small set of servers and were recurrent in nature. While some of them needed capacity related investigation and corrections, some others needed simple alert threshold tuning i.e., changes in thresholds at which alerts get triggered for example: triggering an alert at 65% of CPU utilization rather than 60% considering the role, load and capacity of the server. Through these planned actions, the team was able to reduce the alert volume considerably which saved time and effort involved in handling such incidents both for the monitoring team and for the Wintel team.

All the while both the teams involved were working on those incidents with transactional mindset and due to the overwhelming volume of incidents, did not themselves analyze the causes. They ended up spending time on incidents that were either easily avoidable by fixing the root cause or that deserved no attention. As a result, this caused frequent impact to business from preventable incidents while also losing the team bandwidth on assumed incidents which were not really incidents.

Conclusion

I submit that the importance of problem management cannot be emphasized more. It is the process that focuses on preventive care to improve and maintain the health of the IT estate of an organization by engaging with other IT service management processes and functions as needed. Main purpose of the problem process is preventing incidents and minimizing impact of incidents that cannot be prevented. To achieve this it identifies problems proactively and reactively, advocates preventive care and as required reactive measures as well

II.   Getting familiar- The problem process

- Key terms

As discussed in the first chapter, the problem process focuses on preventive care to improve and maintain the health of the IT estate of an organization by engaging with other IT service management processes and functions as needed. Main purpose of the problem process is preventing incidents and minimizing impact of incidents that cannot be prevented.

Before we move forward, it is important to understand what an incident is and certain other key terms.

Incident

An incident is unplanned unavailability of IT service either partially or fully or degradation of quality of IT service. Example:

- Application not available (for access or for use)

- Application is available but one or more of its functionalities is/ are unavailable
- Application response is slower than agreed performance levels
- One of the 3 servers in a cluster is down. There is no impact on any IT service or business
- Internet or Intranet is not accessible
- Internet or Intranet is slow i.e., network service is slower than agreed performance levels
- Laptop or desktop bluescreen error
- Exchange (email service) not working
- Unable to send/ receive mails

Note- You will note that even when business is not impacted in the above example of a server going down in a cluster of 3 nodes, it is still an incident because an IT component, in this case a server, is not functioning as normal or as usual or as agreed

Incident management

As seen above, an incident refers to something that was functioning earlier but has stopped working now or stopped working as normal. So, someone needs to fix it. Incident management is that process which records such occurrences as incidents and then ensures restoration of such affected IT service or component as quickly as possible. The focus is on time bound or quick restoration to minimize business impact.

Just like a Fire fighting team focuses on dousing the fire as quickly as possible to minimize damage to life and property, the incident management process also focuses on restoring IT service or IT component as quickly as possible.

- **Incident management = Fire fighting**

During incident management, the team may use a temporary solution or a permanent fix depending on availability of the solution(s) and other factors like time needed to implement the solution, business impact due to delay in restoration etc., incident management process does not focus on identifying the root cause or finding a permanent solution rather it focuses on finding (or using) a feasible solution to restore the IT service as soon as possible and minimize business impact.

Problem

A problem is an underlying cause of incident(s). Examples of existence of a problem:

- Occurrence of a major incident
- Same type of incident reported by many users of a specific application or location
- Service desk has observed an increase in a specific type of incident over the last few days/ weeks/ months
- A pattern is observed like network slowness on identified times of day or days of week
- A trend of high utilization of underlying IT components or a trend of lower performance levels of such components or IT services (irrespective of business impact observed)
- Repeat incidents

Wider meaning of a problem

The definition of problem must be understood in a wider sense to also include an underlying cause of one or more potential incidents i.e., incidents that may not have occurred yet but may occur in future. As seen above there may be a trend of high utilization or lower performance levels of certain underlying IT components observed. This may not have impacted any IT service or business yet i.e., incident may not have occurred yet however, when such a trend is observed, raising a problem ticket is necessary for further investigation and remediation to prevent incidents that can potentially be caused by such IT components.

Problem management

Unlike the incident process, the problem process focuses on identifying the root cause of a problem and then implementing corrective actions and preventive actions (CAPA) to permanently fix the root cause. The focus is on permanent resolution of the problem and prevention of occurrence or recurrence of incidents due to the identified root cause

Identifying the root cause needs technical expertise. Sometimes it may even need engaging the Original Equipment Manufacturer (OEM) or principal Vendor of the technology or product like EMC, CISCO, IBM, Microsoft, Oracle etc., So, identifying the root cause is kind of a research process that needs technical expertise

- **Problem management = Research**

Besides identifying the root cause, identifying a permanent solution also may need equally high technical expertise including OEM or principal vendor support. The next logical step after root cause is identified is finding a permanent solution. A permanent solution refers to both corrective and preventive actions (CAPA). Identifying a permanent solution is important because as discussed above, the problem process focuses on fixing the root cause so as to prevent incidents in future just like fire prevention measures like using fire- proof material or material which is low/ not inflammable etc.,

- **Problem management = Fire prevention**

Thus incident management process focuses on firefighting whereas the problem management process focuses on fire prevention.

Workaround

Workaround is a solution that resolves an incident temporarily. It is usually quickly implementable in nature so as to decrease the impact of incident through faster resolution. Sometimes a workaround may be used to decrease the probability of occurrence of an incident and there by decrease the impact of the problem. Example:

- A workaround may be- when user of application 'A' complains of error xx1, please unregister the user and re-register the user as an authorized user of the application. This should resolve the user's incident
- A workaround may be- when a user complains of screen freeze or 'no response' issue with application 'B' while performing a transaction of type 'Trans-x' in the application, manually end the specific transaction from the database end. This should resolve the user's incident

Known error

A problem is called a known error when root cause and/ or workaround are available. I have intentionally used 'or' in the above statement because even when the root cause is not known but only a workaround, it is still beneficial to call a 'problem' as 'known error' and publish it to the relevant IT support teams along with the workaround details so that when they come across an incident caused by this known error, they are able to use the published workaround and resolve the incident.

Known error Database (KEDB)

This is a repository that holds information about all the known errors along with the associated symptoms, root cause, workaround and status of the known error, the related problem record number and status of the problem. This may be maintained in an Excel sheet or in a tool. This is one of the most important outputs of the problem process.

Temporary fix, Permanent fix

A solution that temporarily resolves an incident may be called a temporary fix. Permanent fix is the one that permanently resolves an incident or a problem.

CAPA (corrective actions and preventive actions)

In the realm of quality, corrective action is used to refer to actions that fix or correct an issue whereas preventive actions refer to those actions which prevent occurrence or recurrence of the same issue. Usually in IT service management, corrective actions are used to refer to those actions which resolve an incident whereas preventive actions to those which prevent an incident on the same affected component due to the same cause.

I prefer a slightly modified approach from my experience as a problem manager. I prefer to use 'corrective actions' to refer to those actions which will prevent recurrence of an incident on the same IT component due to the same cause. This means corrective actions include both the actions that permanently fix the cause on the affected IT component and also those actions which are preventive in nature and prevent recurrence of an incident on the same IT component due to the same cause. As you note 'corrective actions' focus on the affected IT component and cover all actions which prevent incident recurrence on the affected IT component. Example:

- The action of applying a patch on a server to permanently fix the cause is a corrective action
- For the same server, establishing a process of regularly checking the need to apply any patches on the server to prevent such incidents in future is also a corrective action

When it comes to 'preventive actions', I prefer to use this to refer to actions that shall prevent recurrence of an incident due to the same root cause on all other IT components in the entire organization that are similar to the affected IT component where corrective actions have been applied. Example:

- The action of applying a patch on a server to permanently fix the cause is a corrective action
- For the same server, establishing a process of regularly checking the need to apply any

patches on the server to prevent such incidents in future is also a corrective action

- In this case, preventive action will include patching all other similar servers in the organization, running the same technology and need patching
- preventive actions will also include establishing a process to regularly check all the servers in the organization for any patching needs to prevent such incidents on any server in future, caused by non-application of required patches

Configuration item (CI)

- Any IT component whose configuration is significant to operation of one or more IT services
- Example: A database, a server, a network link, etc.,
- Hence it is important to control changes to configuration of CIs
- Information about configuration of CIs is maintained in a database called Configuration management database (CMDB)

As we know, the main purpose of the problem process is preventing incidents and minimizing impact of incidents that cannot be prevented. To achieve this, it identifies problems proactively and also reactively, advocates preventive care and as required reactive measures as well

Key stages or phases of the problem process are:

- Problem identification
- Problem investigation - Root cause analysis
- Problem resolution – Provide workaround and permanent solution
- Problem closure

Key inputs of the problem process are:

- Incident data
- Monitoring data including alerts, performance trends
- Known errors from development teams, vendors and KEDB
- User feedback (transaction or ticket CSAT)
- OEM or Vendor identified problems (Ex: Bugs)

- Suspected problems reported by any staff involved in IT service management
- Suspected problems reported by customer (/business) or users

Key Outputs of the problem process are:

- Root cause
- workaround
- Updated KEDB (known error Database)
- Permanent Solution
- Request for change
- Identified risks

Key customers awaiting the above outputs:

- Incident management process and staff
- Service Desk
- Users (who need a permanent solution to their recurring IT issues)
- Customer (/ business) who always desires a stable IT environment devoid of disruptions

A high level view of the problem process:

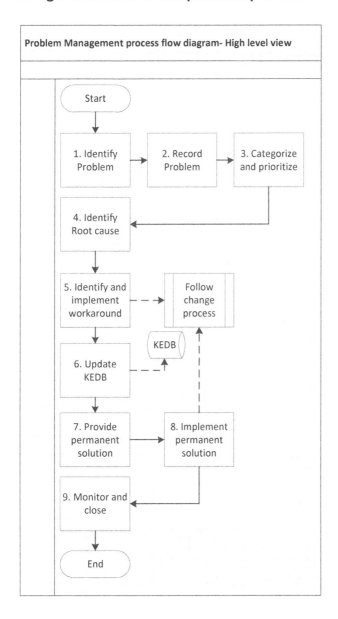

Problem Management process flow diagram- High level view

Start

1. Identify Problem → 2. Record Problem → 3. Categorize and prioritize

4. Identify Root cause

5. Identify and implement workaround ⇢ Follow change process

KEDB

6. Update KEDB

7. Provide permanent solution → 8. Implement permanent solution

9. Monitor and close

End

Problem process steps from the above high level process flow diagram:

1. Identify problem

This is an important activity as it triggers the rest of the process activities and helps prevent incidents. A problem may be identified proactively or reactively.

- **Reactive-**
  - A problem is said to be identified reactively if the problem process is initiated to find the root cause and permanent solution of an incident that has occurred, usually a major or high priority incident. Similarly a reactive problem may also be identified when users or service desk or incident management team or IT support staff identify without any data analysis some recurring incidents indicating a potential problem
- **Proactive-**
  - A problem is said to be identified proactively when the said problem is discovered through analysis of incidents or monitoring data, analysis of utilization and

performance statistics, information sourced from Vendors and Project (development or deployment) teams and any other proactive measures

- **Preventive** problem management activities focuses on certain measures that can be taken by the problem manager and the technology teams to prevent incidents

2. Record problem (problem recording)

It is necessary that all the available information regarding the identified problem be recorded to aid root cause analysis. Typically information to be recorded includes,

- Problem description- statement describing the symptoms observed by users or IT support staff
- Impact-
  - o Details of impact like the number of users or business services or IT services or IT applications or IT components or locations affected by the problem
  - o Where other impact information like revenue loss or potential revenue loss or

safety threat to life or property. Any compliance, legal, statutory or regulatory consequences known should also be included as part of the impact details of the problem

- Suspected or known cause(s), if any
- Available or potential resolution, if any, whether temporary or permanent including workaround
- Related incidents-
  - It is important to link all the relevant incidents suspected to have a common root cause to the problem record being raised/ created
  - Thereafter, every incident suspected to be due to the same problem must also be diligently linked to the same problem record
  - Linking may be in the ticketing tool in the form of relationship between such incidents and the problem record or as fields in the incident and problem forms in the tool
  - Or linking may be manual i.e., entering all the incident numbers in the work log of the problem record and vice versa, the

problem record number in all those
incidents

- Chronology of events from incident detection
  to resolution, for incidents already resolved
- Any Vendor provided information like hot fix,
  or cause/ bug information etc.,
- Major incident report, where relevant must
  be included as part of the problem record

Typically, this information must be recorded in
the ticket when creating the problem record

3. **Categorize and Prioritize**

- **Categorize**- It is important to categorize the
  problem for routing and also to use this data
  for future analysis. It is recommended that
  the same categorization scheme be used for
  both incidents and problems. There is no
  need to have different categorization
  schemes for incidents and problems because
  categorization is meant to facilitate routing
  based on the service or component impacted
  and not based on the type of ticket (incident
  or problem)
  - o Usually, three- level categorization is
    observed for both incidents and problem

and it is commonly known as (Category> Type> Item) **CTI**. Here, Category, Type and Item are three fields in the ticketing tool used to categorize the problem

- ○ The three fields may be called by different names in different ticketing tools like Category> Area> Sub Area or Category> Type> Sub type or Opcat1> Opcat2> Opcat3 etc., the essence still remains i.e., to categorize the problem into three levels
- ○ Examples of CTI (not exhaustive)-
  - Workstation> access> password reset
  - Workstation> access> account unlock
  - Workstation> security> AV update
  - Workstation> security> AV install
  - Workstation> software> install/ renew
  - Collaboration> lync> not opening
  - Collaboration> outlook> unable to send/ receive
  - Collaboration> outlook> hang or no response
  - business application> SalesForce> password reset
  - business application> SalesForce> no response

- Corporate application> payroll > not opening
- Corporate application> payroll > no response
- Corporate application> performance > no response
- Infrastructure> storage> SAN issue
- Infrastructure> storage> SAN allocation
- Infrastructure> storage> Array errors
- Infrastructure> backup> job failure
- Infrastructure> backup> tape drive issue
- Infrastructure> backup> restore
- Server> Windows> disk space
- Server> Windows> local admin
- Server> Windows> not reachable
- Server> Unix> local admin
- Network> link> bandwidth
- Network> link> packet drops
- Network> link> down
- Network> link> flap
- Network> link> CRC errors
- Network> internet> slow
- Network> internet> no connectivity
- Network> internet> connectivity issues
- Network> intranet> connectivity issues

- Network> intranet> slow
- Network> intranet> no connectivity
- Network> router> down
- Network> router> interface issue/ error
- Network> switch> down
- Network> switch> port issue
- Network security> Firewall> down
- Network security> Firewall> high CPU
- Network security> Firewall> high memory
- Network security> Firewall> modify rules
- Network security> Firewall> rules issue
- Network security> IPS/ IDS> alarm
- Infrastructure> database> down/ no response
- Infrastructure> database> transaction error
- Infrastructure> database> query not running
- Infrastructure> database> read/ write error
- Database> Oracle> log file issue
- Infrastructure> VM> host down

- **Prioritize**- It is important to prioritize the problem based on its impact and urgency so that immediate attention is given to problems with higher priority just as it is done in case of incidents. This approach of prioritization helps minimize business impact by resolving problems with higher priority i.e., with higher impact and/ or urgency first

Sample Priority Matrix	Urgency-High	Urgency-Medium	Urgency-Low
Impact-High	Priority 1 (P1)	Priority 2 (P2)	Priority 3 (P3)
Impact-Medium	Priority 2 (P2)	Priority 3 (P3)	Priority 4 (P4)
Impact-Low	Priority 3 (P3)	Priority 4 (P4)	Priority 5 (P5)

After a problem has been categorized and prioritized, it is assigned to a problem owner from a relevant technology team for investigation of the root cause.

Identify Root cause

Root cause analysis activity fundamentally differentiates the problem process from the incident process.

- This activity focuses on identifying the root cause of the problem so that the root cause can be fixed to prevent incidents in future due to the same cause
- Root cause analysis is performed by the problem owner engaging as needed, the principal technology vendor or other technology teams
- Root cause analysis is performed by a senior engineer (Level 2) or a Subject Matter Expert (SME/ Level 3) and not by a junior engineer
- Popular RCA techniques include
  - 5-Why analysis
  - Fishbone analysis (also known as Cause-effect analysis)
  - Fault tree analysis

4. Identify and implement workaround

As the problem owner starts working on the problem, apart from root cause analysis, in parallel, he/ she will also work towards identifying a workaround.

- A workaround is a solution that either provides a temporary solution to the incidents caused by the problem or decreases the probability of occurrence of an incident due to the problem identified
- A workaround is usually by nature quickly implementable for speedier resolution of incidents caused by the problem
- It is important to provide the workaround to incident management staff for their use to resolve incidents caused by the problem
- Sometimes the problem owner may engage the required teams and implement the workaround to decrease the probability of occurrence of incidents
- In either case, it is important to follow the organization's change management process to implement the workaround i.e., as needed, raise a change request and seek required

approvals before implementing the workaround

- Sometimes it may also be necessary to seek approval from customer or business stakeholders before implementing a workaround

5. Update KEDB

As discussed above it is important to communicate the workaround to incident management staff for their use to resolve incidents caused by the problem. For this purpose, a database called known error Database is maintained.

- By definition, a problem is called a known error when both root cause and workaround are known
- However, based on experience as problem manager and considering the importance of communicating known error information, I recommend that as soon as workaround is known irrespective of whether the root cause is known or not, the problem be designated a known error

- Known errors are maintained in a database called known error database (KEDB)
- Whenever a known error is discovered, KEDB is updated with details of the known error which at minimum includes details of the symptoms reported by users, the workaround identified, the root cause identified, number of incidents resolved using the known error, the associated problem ticket, status of the known error, status of the problem ticket
- All the incident management staff from the technology teams must have access to KEDB so that they are able to identify and apply suitable workaround to provide faster incident resolution

6. Provide permanent solution

Besides workaround it is essential to provide a permanent solution, only then can the objective of problem management process i.e., prevent incident occurrence or recurrence, be achieved

- A solution is said to be a permanent solution if it fixes the root cause permanently

- To identify a permanent solution, the problem owner may need support from other technical teams or from principal vendor of the product or technology and must engage such teams as necessary
- Usually a permanent solution will need a change to one or more configuration items

7. **Implement permanent solution**
   - As discussed above a permanent solution will usually need a change to one or more configuration items
   - it is important to follow the organization's change management process to implement the permanent solution i.e., as needed, raise a change request and seek required approvals before implementing the workaround
   - Sometimes it may also be necessary to seek approval from customer or business stakeholders before implementing the permanent solution

8. Monitor and close

Monitor-

- After implementing the permanent solution, the problem manager must monitor the effectiveness for a defined period
- The defined period may be static i.e., a fixed period for all problems where a permanent solution is implemented or it may vary by problem from a few days to a few weeks or months depending on the problem
- During the monitoring period, problem manager should try to identify if any incident has occurred due to the same cause. If yes, it indicates that the permanent solution may not have been effective and that the problem may need further investigation

Close-

- After it is clear that the permanent solution implemented has been successful in arresting incident occurrence or recurrence during the monitoring period, the problem is ready to be closed
- After the successful monitoring, a problem may be directly marked 'closed' or may be

marked as 'resolved' with auto-closure after 2 days or as per organizational needs

- Sometimes, a problem may be closed even without a permanent solution being implemented. Such cases may be when root cause itself is not known or permanent solution is either not identified or not implementable. Such cases will be discussed in detail in later chapters

Thus the problem process identifies a problem both proactively and reactively and works towards providing a workaround and a permanent solution for the same

III.   Identifying the problem

As discussed above, a problem may be identified proactively or reactively. A problem is said to be identified proactively when the said problem is discovered through data analysis. It may be through

- Analysis of incident data,
- Analysis of monitoring data,
- Analysis of utilization and performance statistics,
- Information sourced from Vendors,
- Information sourced from Project (development or deployment) teams and
- Any other proactive measure

Analysis of incident data (CTI analysis)

Analysis of incidents means identifying patterns or potential problems using incident data i.e., using data captured during incident management. Typically this data to be analysed is captured as 'fields' in the incident form of the ticketing tool.

Various types of incident data analysis useful in problem identification are:

- CTI analysis
- Resolution code based analysis
- CI based analysis
- incident description based analysis

For the purpose of our study, we shall focus on CTI analysis because other analysis listed above may be used as part of CTI analysis to identify potential problems

As discussed in 'Overview of the problem process' section of chapter 2, problems are categorized for the purpose of routing to the correct team. The same is true of incidents. incidents are categorized so that they are routed to the correct team for resolution. It is recommended that the same categorization scheme be used for both incidents and problems. There is no need to have different categorization schemes for incidents and problems because categorization is meant to facilitate routing based on the service or component impacted and not based on the type of ticket (incident or problem)

- Usually, three- level categorization is observed for both incidents and problem and it is commonly known as (Category> Type> Item) CTI categorization scheme. Category, Type and Item are three fields in the ticketing tool used to categorize the incident or problem
- The three fields may be called by different names in different ticketing tools like Category> Area> Sub Area or Category> Type> Sub type or Opcat1> Opcat2> Opcat3 etc., the essence still remains i.e., to categorize the incident or problem into three levels

Analysis of incident data, also known as CTI analysis is performed to identify potential problems based on categorization of incidents. The incident data may be analyzed to identify potential problems using the following steps:

1. **Gather incident data**

Gather incident data, ideally 3 months data that should at a minimum include

- Incident source (monitoring tool, user, etc.,)
- Incident priority

- Fields used for categorization (CTI),
- Resolver group (last team that holds the incident ownership),
- Incident description,
- CI impacted,
- User and/ or location impacted,
- Resolution code,
- Incident date

2. Analyze data

a) <u>Basic Pivot</u>- As a first step, gather incident data listed above in a Microsoft Excel spreadsheet and create a Pivot table and segregate incidents based on source i.e., incidents caused by monitoring tool alerts and incidents from other sources. This step is important because depending on the source, for each set of incidents analysis steps will be slightly different. Sample result of such a Pivot is shown below

Count of Incident Number	
Incident source	Total
Alert	1200
Other	6200
Grand Total	7400

How to do this in Excel?

- o Use shortcut keys Alt+ d+ p+ f in the spreadsheet containing the gathered incident data to create a Pivot table
- o Then, add the field containing the incident source in the 'Row labels' section of the Pivot fields list pop-up dialog box in Excel
- o Then, add incident number/ ID field in the 'Values' section of the dialog box.
- o The screenshot below shows how to create a Pivot table with fields discussed above

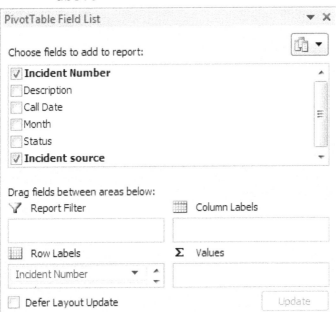

b) <u>CTI for alert- triggered incidents</u>- Second step is to focus on alert- triggered incidents which will usually be lower in volume as compared to incidents from other sources.
  - For this, apply a filter in the Pivot table to include only the alert triggered incidents
  - Now, modify the same Pivot to segregate alert- triggered incidents by category, type, item and CI
  - This should result in Pivot table with data as shown in the sample below

Count of incidents				
Category	Type	Item	CI	Total
Hardware	Server	CPU	server 1	70
			server 2	50
			server 3	30
			server 4	20
			others	80
		CPU total		250
		disk	server 2	30
			server 3	25
			server 4	25
			server 8	20
			others	50
		disk total		150
		memory	server 4	30
			server 1	25
			server 3	25
			others	20
		memory total		100
	Server Total			540
	Printer			10
Hardware Total				550
Storage	Back up failure	job failure		40

How to do this in Excel?

- o You can see the 'Pivot fields list' dialog box by just using the right mouse click anywhere in the Pivot table and selecting the option 'show field list'
- o Move the incident source field to 'report filter' section of the Pivot fields list dialog box in Excel spreadsheet just like 'incident type' field in the below figure
- o Then add category, type, item and CI fields to the row labels section just like 'category' and 'subcategory' fields shown in the below figure

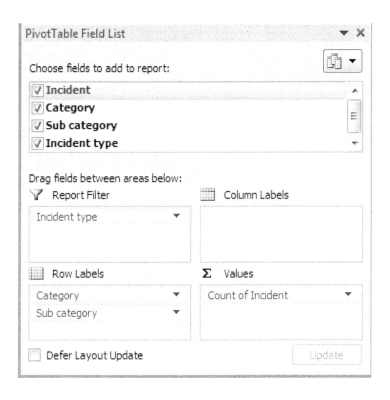

c) <u>CIs with repeat incidents</u>- Now, look for configuration items (servers, databases, routers, links etc.,) with repeat incidents

- o You may record each such CI with repeat incidents as an issue or potential problem area, have a preliminary discussion with the respective technology SME and then raise a problem record for all such cases where there is a problem suspected or where a need for further investigation is established

- o In the sample data shown above in step 2b, each of the servers 1, 2, 3, 4 and 8 have repeat alerts for different kinds of issues like CPU, memory, unavailability (down) and disk space

- o From this data, 13 potential problem areas highlighted in the below sample data, can be pursued through discussions with the respective technology teams and then problem records can be created for those servers and issues which need further investigation

- o At this stage one may also add another 'resolution code' field to the row label to identify spurious, false or duplicate alert volume, record such issues as problem records and discuss remedial actions with the technology teams to decrease such alert volume through alert tuning (changing alert parameters or alert thresholds at which incidents are triggered)

Count of incidents				
Category	Type	Item	CI	Total
Hardware	Server	CPU	server 1	70
			server 2	50
			server 3	30
			server 4	20
			others	80
		CPU total		250
		disk	server 2	30
			server 3	25
			server 4	25
			server 8	20
			others	50
		disk total		150
		memory	server 4	30
			server 1	25
			server 3	25
			others	20
		memory total		100
	Server Total			540
	Printer			10

d) <u>CIs from alert description</u>- In the above step 2b, you may find that CI data is sometimes not available as a separate field. This is because there may be ticketing systems which still do not allow CI to be mapped to incidents in the incident module/ form

   o If configuration item (CI) data is not available as a separate field then CI name must be first extracted from 'incident description' of alert- triggered incidents, into a separate column in the same Excel sheet where incident data is gathered

   o After which, step 2b and step 2c discussed above must be applied to incidents potential problems from alert- triggered incidents i.e., identify CIs with repeat incidents

   o Success of this step depends on inclusion of CI name in the incident description of all the alert- triggered incidents. Also on use of a standard description format so that 'text to column' functionality of Excel can be easily used

How to do this in Excel?

- o CI name can be extracted from incident description using 'Text to column' functionality in the Excel spreadsheet where alert- triggered incidents are listed
- o You are advised to read about how to use this Excel functionality. It is fairly simple although it may be time consuming if you are dealing with high volume of alert-triggered incidents

e) <u>Non-alert incidents</u>- Now, let's look at incidents not triggered by alerts. In the sample data shown above in step 2a, you note over 6000 incidents with source marked as 'other' i.e., are not triggered by alerts. Filter out alert- triggered incidents and retain the rest

How to do this in Excel?

- o You can see the 'Pivot fields list' dialog box by just using the right mouse click anywhere in the Pivot table and selecting the option 'show field list'
- o Move the 'incident source' field, into 'report filter' section of the 'Pivot fields

list' dialog box in Excel, and retain only incidents not triggered by alerts.

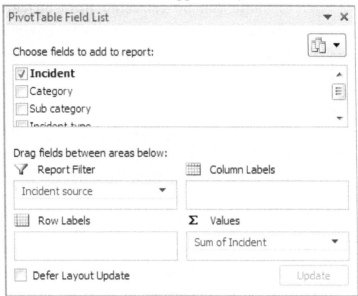

f) <u>CTI for incidents</u>- Now, update the Pivot table by adding fields corresponding to Category, type and item to the row labels

   o Sort the resultant count of incidents in descending (decreasing) order so that in each bucket (category> type> item) the combination with highest number of incidents is on top

   o The resultant sample data may look as shown below

- Select the top contributors within each CTI combination for further analysis
- The below sample data does not include 'item' only includes 'category' and ' type' fields

Count of incidents		
Category	Type	Total
Hardware	Laptop	300
	Handheld	250
	Server	200
	Printer	180
	Desktop	90
	Monitor	80
	RSA Hardtoken	50
	Scanner	10
	VC Equipment	8
	Keyboard	8
	Mouse	2
Hardware Total		1178
Workstation	Outlook	700
	Exchange	100
	IE	100
	Adobe	70
	Excel	50
	Citrix	20
	OS- Win7	15
	Symantec	12

How to do this in Excel?

o You can see the 'Pivot fields list' dialog box
   by just using the right mouse click
   anywhere in the Pivot table and selecting
   the option 'show field list'
o Add category, type and item one after the
   other in the row labels section of the
   'Pivot fields list' dialog box in the Excel
   spreadsheet

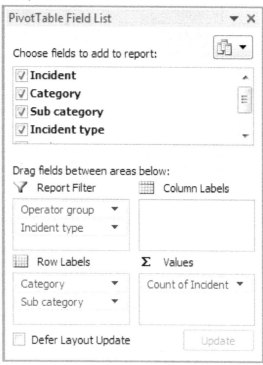

o   Once done, use the left mouse click on the arrow shown against the row label 'Category' of the Pivot table and choose 'more sort options'

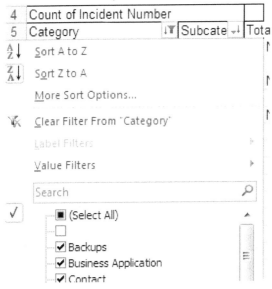

○ After choosing 'more options', choose descending order by count of incidents as shown below

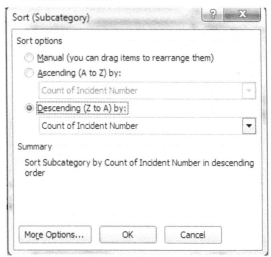

○ REPEAT the above 2 steps of sorting the data in descending order for the other two row labels of 'type' and 'item'

g) CIs with repeat incidents and use of 'resolution code'- Where CI information is available, adding CI information as row label will easily highlight potential problem areas which can be taken up for discussion with the respective technology teams as discussed above in step 2c for problem identification and creating problem records. Sample data is shown below

- o At this stage, ' resolution code' field can also be added as a 'row label' in the Pivot fields list to identify set of incidents in each CTI bucket that have been marked as 'user education/ 'how to' / informed user' all such issues can be explored to be recorded as problems with remedial action being user education
- o Also above step may highlight those incidents with 'resolved using workaround or temporary solution' as resolution code. All such issues must be verified against the problem records and any such issue is not already pursued as problem record, a problem record must be created as discussed in step 2c above
- o Success of this step depends on having a streamlined/ useful set of 'resolution code values' and also educating the incident management team on their usage

Count of Incident Number			
Category	Type	CI	Total
Hardware	Laptop	INZ4441	100
		INZ4567	80
		INZ5432	60
		INZ5741	4
		INZ5782	4
		and so on....	
	Laptpo Total		300
	Handheld		250
	Server	server 6	100
		server 8	50
		server 1	20
		server 3	10
		server 22	6
		server 22	4
		server 14	2
		so on....	
	Server Total		200

h) <u>incident description and other fields</u>- Apart from configuration item and resolution code, other fields like user, location and even incident description can be used for analysis to identify potential problem areas

- o Same users affected by same incidents repeatedly can be identified by adding 'user details' field as a row label to the Pivot table above instead of CI field in the above step 2g

- o Manually identifying specific keywords from 'incident description' field of the incidents from each CTI bucket in the above table can also highlight potential problem areas. Ex: 'voicemail password' or 'VPN issue' or 'application x screen freeze' may be keywords found repeatedly indicating potential problems

- o These issues must be discussed as mentioned above in step 2c with the respective technology team to identify and record problems for investigation

i) CI based analysis- Where configuration item information is available in the incident data, 'configuration item' field can be added to Row labels of the Pivot table ahead of 'category' field in the step 2f mentioned above

- o This will highlight configuration items with repeat incidents which can be further analyzed using CTI analysis discussed above in steps 2f and 2g

Analysis of monitoring data and Analysis of utilization and performance statistics

Analysis of incidents triggered by monitoring alerts has been discussed in the above section in steps 2a to 2d. This section focuses on monitoring data like utilization and performance trends and alerts that are not ticketed (Ex: warning alerts, informational alerts)

- Repeat alerts- One can look at monitoring data in an Excel sheet and apply Pivot as discussed above to identify configuration items on which repeat alerts are seen. Such occurrences should be discussed with respective technology teams as mentioned above in step 2c for identifying problem areas. The focus is on those alerts which have not resulted in alert- triggered incidents
  - As an example if 70% CPU utilization on a server is the threshold set for an automatic alert- triggered incident and 65% for only a warning alert in the monitoring tool/ console without an automatic incident, there can be many situations in which there may be 10/ 20 or

30 warning alerts without a single automatic incident i.e., a server CPU utilization may reach 65% 30 times without even once breaching the 70% mark. Such cases will not be identified from alert- triggered incidents analyzed in the previous section. Hence it is important to analyze monitoring data beyond alert-triggered incidents. Sample shown below

o For this to work, CI name/ ID should be available with every monitoring alert either as separate field or as part of alert description. Where CI name is not captured as a separate field, it must be extracted from 'monitoring alert description' using 'Text to column' functionality of Excel as mentioned above in step 2d

Alert type	Alert level	CI	No. of alerts
Server CPU	Warning- 65%	server 42	20
Server CPU	Warning- 65%	server 56	40
Server CPU	Warning- 65%	server 31	25
Link bandwidth	Warning- 85%	Link 1 - ATT	100
Link bandwidth	Warning- 85%	Link 3 - Bharti	65
Link bandwidth	Warning- 85%	Link 2- BT	80
Server disk space	Warning- 80%	server 56	32
Server disk space	Warning- 80%	server 1	54
Server disk space	Warning- 80%	server 24	26

- <u>Utilization and performance trends</u>- This data from the monitoring tools should be used to identify any adverse trends and take them up for discussion with the respective technology teams as explained above in step 2c
  - From the discussions if there are any devices found with a potential underlying problem or if a need is established for further investigation into the trend observed, a problem record must be created
  - Typical trends to look for are listed below (not exhaustive, more parameters can be identified by engaging the respective technology SMEs)

- CPU, memory trends (average, peak) for all relevant IT components like servers, routers, switches etc.,
- Disk space trends for servers
- DB size growth rate for databases
- I/O rates, free space and data growth rate for storage devices
- Network link bandwidth utilization (peak and average)
- Application response time trends
- Forecast trends- Some monitoring tools are also able to provide 30, 60, 90 days forecast of the likely utilization trends in future which is Excellent data to easily identify potential problem areas

Information sourced from Vendors

- It is important to gather Vendor published information like known errors, workarounds, bugs, hot fixes etc., for their products (hardware or software). This may be gathered by subscribing to Vendor bulletins, vendor notifications and other communication channels like industry fora, technology/ professional community, Vendor website etc.,

- Whenever such information is found of value to the IT support team, the same must be captured as a known error in the KEDB with details of the bug or error and the workaround provided by the Vendor. The information must also be captured as a problem record which should be referenced to by the known errors recorded so that the lifecycle of that problem identified by the Vendor can be tracked until closure, for internal purposes

- Problem manager may have to depend on technology teams to actively pursue Vendor provided information mentioned above

Information sourced from project teams (development and deployment teams)

- Just like information sourced from Vendors, it is important for the problem manager to develop a good rapport and hold regular reviews with the release and deployment team and the Testing team
- These reviews should focus on gathering information about defects identified in testing and their status
    - Any defects being finally moved into production must be captured as known errors in the KEDB with details of the bug or error and the workaround provided by the development team
    - Support teams must be adequately trained on such workarounds
- Also, every such known errors must be related to a problem ticket which should be used to track such defects moved into production until their closure/ resolution
- Such problem tickets should be discussed by the problem manager with the development team periodically until defect resolution

Any other proactive measure

- Besides the above discussed sources, if information about a potential underlying problem is brought to the notice of the problem manager by any other individual part of IT services provider organization or business or user or any other Vendor, the problem manager must take note of such problems and engage relevant technology teams to understand the need for further investigation and accordingly raise problem ticket for the same

- Reactive

As discussed in the 'overview of the problem process' section of chapter 2, a problem is said to be identified reactively if the problem process is initiated to find the root cause and permanent solution of an incident without any proactive data analysis being carried out to identify the problem. Typically a reactive problem may be recorded through the following ways:`

- Mapping every major incident to a problem record to find the root cause and permanent solution
- Mapping every high priority incident to a problem record to find the root cause and permanent solution
- Mapping repeat incidents where incidents may be of medium or low priority to problem record to find the root cause and permanent solution
  - Such recurrence itself may be identified as part of daily support activities by the Service Desk or any IT support staff without any data analysis or

- May be identified and reported by business or users

- Preventive

Apart from proactive and reactive approach to problem identification, there are also some precautions that the problem manager can take or drive in the IT team which can help prevent incidents.

- Such preventive activities driven by the problem manager to prevent incidents may be termed as preventive approach to problem management
- Some of the preventive activities listed below may actually result in the problem manager participating in or engaging with other IT service management processes to ensure that some of those process activities are carried out as expected or carried out effectively
- Preventive approach may include preventive activities like the ones mentioned below. It is not an exhaustive list; one may add any other preventive measure to this list to suit their organizational needs!

- Attending **change control meeting** to ensure that the proposed changes are
  - adequately tested
  - Tested in a test environment that is in synch with production environment
  - Test cases used have been certified as relevant and adequate
  - Test results have been signed off as satisfactory
  - Test defects being moved into production are agreed with business/ customer
  - Such test defects have been captured in the known error database (KEDB)
  - Customer/ business approval is in place for the change activity where needed
  - Change roll back plan is tested or is a proven method
- **Engage with availability management process**
  - To ensure that all the start/ stop/ recovery procedures are clearly documented
  - Staff are aware of existence of such procedure documents and are conversant with such procedures

- To ensure that single points of failure that can lead to incidents (or unavailability) are recorded as *risks* and discussed with relevant stakeholders including customer and risk response (i.e., accept, mitigate or reject) is recorded
  - **Engage with release and deployment management process/ team**
    - To ensure that anything moved into production is verified against an acceptance checklist and is signed off as supportable by relevant IT support teams including the Service Desk

Conclusion

- The objective of this chapter is to help readers understand various ways in which problems can be identified to prevent incident occurrence or recurrence
- As you have discovered, a problem may be identified proactively through data gathering and analysis or reactively when an underlying problem is identified as a result of one or more incidents without any data analysis. One

may also take a preventive approach which may include engaging with other teams and other IT service management processes to ensure that some of their critical activities are performed effectively so as to prevent incident occurrence

IV.   What's causing it?

-   Root cause analysis (symptoms Vs cause)

As discussed in the very first chapter, It is important to understand the underlying causes, faults or errors in the IT infrastructure, application and other components like processes, people skills, technology etc., which support delivery of IT services so that we are able to avoid occurrence or at least recurrence of incidents

Just like a Doctor not only gives medication for immediate relief of symptoms like pain or fever but also tries to identify the root cause through various medical tests (like blood test, X-ray etc.,) and tries to treat the cause so that the patient is permanently relieved of the symptoms (i.e., no recurrence of the symptoms like pain, fever etc.,) due to the identified cause, it is important for IT support teams to not only use a workaround or temporary solution to resolve incidents but also identify the root cause of incidents and fix the same permanently to avoid incident recurrence. Similarly just like vaccinations are taken as a preventive measure to prevent specific diseases, certain proactive and preventive measures must be taken to identify problems proactively and fix them so as to prevent occurrence of incidents in the first place.

Example: Consider an incident where an application is unavailable because database is not responding

- The Database technology team identifies space crunch caused by log files and then they clear log files as an immediate action to resolve the incident
- It is important at this stage for the Database team to understand and fix the cause of the problem
- Is storing the log files required? If no (not required), can the same be disabled for the database in question?
- If yes (required), can there be a monitoring alert when the free space is less than a specific threshold say 30% against which a script can automatically clear the log files on the affected database?
- This will solve the problem permanently on the affected database but not in the entire IT estate

- So, the same checks regarding the storage of log files must be performed for all other databases in the organization
- As relevant, either logging must be disabled or monitoring log file size coupled with automatic clearance of log files, must be set up on all the databases
- This will solve the problem permanently i.e., fix the identified cause in the entire organization

In the above example, the process/ steps/ activity of identifying the cause is called 'root cause analysis', studied in this chapter and the activity of permanently solving the cause from leading to any more incidents in the organization is called ' fixing the problem' studied in the next chapter.

I believe the above example has cemented in your mind, the need to perform root cause analysis. From the 'Overview of the problem process' section of chapter 2, we understand that after a problem is identified, it is recorded i.e., certain information is captured, it is then categorized and prioritized and assigned to a problem owner from the relevant technology team.

The problem owner is expected to perform root cause analysis. For this purpose, he/ she gathers information recorded in the problem ticket and all the associated incidents and begins a technical investigation. This may involve gathering and analysis of technical information like logs etc., analysis of chronology of events from incident detection to resolution, this may also need assistance from SMEs/ architects or even the principal vendor of the technology like Cisco, Microsoft, IBM etc.,

The output of all this analysis is identifying the 'root cause' which is the source or cause of the problem and leading to occurrence of incident(s).

- 'How to'- RCA techniques and RCA
  template

While the technology SMEs are able to find the root cause through technical investigation and diagnosis, many a time customer is invariably not happy with the quality of the root cause published and I had experienced the same in several accounts that I was engaged with to drive problem management.

A closer look reveals absence of a structured approach to root cause analysis among the technology teams and also sometimes a poorly documented root cause which is unable to show a connection between the problem (related incidents), the identified cause and the proposed corrective and preventive actions. This issue can be easily resolved using any of the popular root cause analysis techniques and also by creating a root cause analysis template for the technology teams to document and present the root cause to the customer.

Root cause analysis (RCA) techniques

RCA techniques allow technology teams to have a structured approach to/ during their technical investigation to find the root cause. Some of the popular RCA techniques are:

- '5-why' analysis
- Fishbone or Cause- Effect analysis (Ishikawa diagram)
- Fault tree analysis
- Pareto analysis (which is more useful for problem identification or segregating the top causes from trivial many)
- Kepner- Tregoe analysis

All the technical staff must be trained on at least the first three RCA techniques listed above. Let's examine those three techniques.

'5-Why' analysis

This is one of the simplest and widely used techniques for root cause analysis. It is useful not only in the context of IT services but also in general in all walks of life. Most of us use this technique either knowingly or otherwise in both our work and life in general.

This technique involves asking the first 'why' (what caused the problem or incident or issue in question). Response to which must be questioned by another 'why' (second 'why') and so on until one is convinced that the root cause has been identified. Example:

- Consider the issue discussed in the first chapter of Mr. Iyer regularly struggling to reach the bus on time. Now applying the '5-why' analysis, you may ask,
  - First why- Why does Mr. Iyer struggle frequently to reach the bus on time
    - Response- He does not wake up on time
  - Second why- Why does he fail to wake up on time?
    - Response- He forgets to set the alarm or is unable to respond to the alarm
  - Third why- Why does this happen?
    - Response- He has not made a habit (i.e., does not follow a process) of setting the alarm without fail or even if

he sets the alarm, he is late to bed and hence unable to respond to the alarm due to inadequate sleep
- o Fourth why- Why does he get late to bed?
  - ▪ Response- He either does not plan early bed time (i.e., absence of process) or lacks discipline to stick to the plan (i.e., lack or failure of process controls)
- It is clear that the root cause is lack of habit (process) and discipline (process controls) to ensure early bed time with the wake- up alarm set to allow for adequate time in the morning to get to the bus without struggle

Let's consider an IT example:

- Consider the incident discussed in the first section of this chapter of application unavailability because of database issue. Now applying the '5-why' analysis, you may ask,
  - o First why- Why is the application not available?
    - ▪ Response- Database is not responding
  - o Second why- Why is the database not responding?

- Response- Space crunch
  - Third Why- Why is the database experiencing space crunch?
    - Response- (Large) Log file size
  - Fourth Why- Why has the log file size grown to a level that it causes space crunch?
    - Response- Lack of process for monitoring and cleanup of log files and lack of process to validate the necessity of log files
- Thus the root cause is identified as- a) lack of event management process for monitoring the log file size with timely alerting and remedial action to prevent incidents and b) lack of process to determine the need to capture log files and accordingly ensure the same is not enabled where log files are not needed to be captured
- **Note**:- Tips and caution related to '5- why' analysis-
  - When asking 'why', focus must not be on blaming individuals but on highlighting process gaps or product defects or technology limitations

- The '5' in the '5-why' analysis is not set in stone, sometimes it may take fewer while sometimes it may take higher number of 'why' questions to get to the root cause
- This works well for simple problems but for something more complex '5-why' may have to be used in combination with Fishbone analysis or Fault tree analysis discussed below

Fishbone or Cause- Effect analysis (Ishikawa diagram)

- This technique provides six areas and encourages one to think through all the possible causes in each of the six areas which may be causing the problem or issue being investigated
- This is an extremely useful technique as it allows one to think through all possible causes of a problem or issue
- The six areas to think through for identifying causes are popularly called 5M and 1E. In the IT services environment, they may be treated as:

- Machine (Product or technology related causes like bugs, limitations, defects, etc.,)
- Man (People related causes like competency or skill set, staff adequacy/ head count)
- Material (Information related causes like inadequate, inaccurate information or more information causing issues)
- Measurements (Reports and review related causes like lack of reporting or reviews)
- Methods (Processes related causes like process not defined, low awareness etc.,)
- External or Environmental factors (any external cause i.e., out of organization control like vendor related issues, business need, natural disasters, political situations, etc.,)

- When investigating a problem, one is encouraged to identify causes under each of the above six areas that may be potentially leading to the issue or problem at hand

How to perform a Fishbone analysis?

- **Step 1**- Document the problem or issue in a horizontal box drawn to right edge of a paper and vertically aligned in the middle as shown below

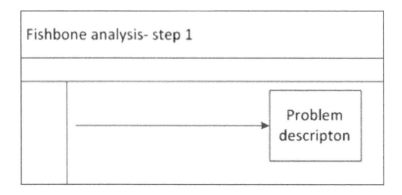

- **Step 2**- Draw six branches for the above six areas (or the one's applicable from the above six areas) emerging from the horizontal line (spine of the Fish) as shown below

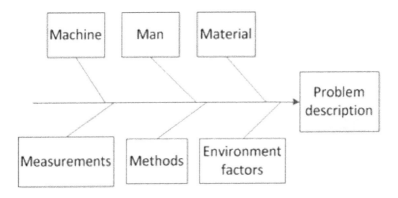

- **Step 3**- Document high level causes under each of these areas and represent them in boxes connected to the branches holding the respective main cause area, as shown below

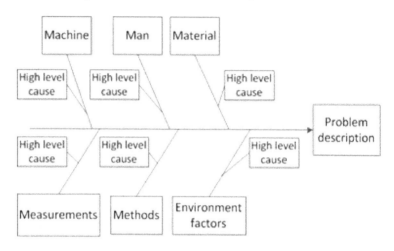

- **Step 4**- Like we observed in the 5-why, ask 'why' for each of the high level causes to identify the reasons or causes for each of the high level causes. Capture these secondary causes in boxes that are connected to the branches of high level causes as shown below

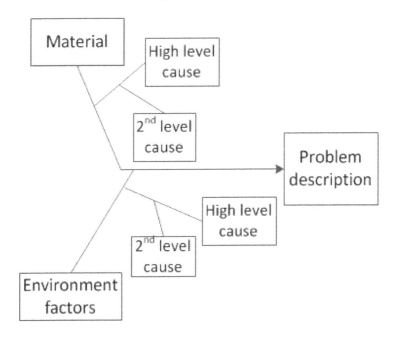

- **Step 5**- Like in the step 4 above; ask 'why' to identify the factors or causes for each of the second level causes. Capture these third level causes in boxes emerging from the branches of the second level causes as shown below

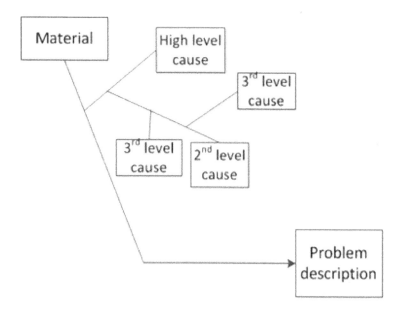

- **Step 6**- Like in the step 5 above; ask 'why' to determine the causes for each of the third level causes and capture them as fourth level causes in boxes emerging from the branches of the third level causes as shown below. This iteration can go on until one is convinced that the root cause under each of the areas has been identified

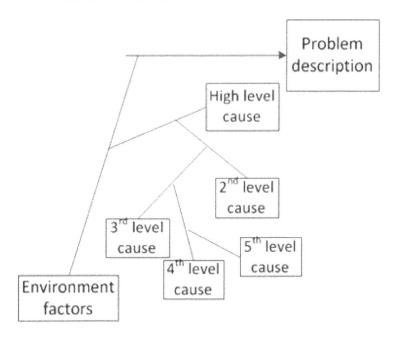

- Thus you observe that '5-why' analysis is inherently used as part of fishbone analysis
- The completed diagram traces causes from lowest level to their effects which are causes that are one level higher and in that manner all the way up to the problem or issue at hand. Hence it is called the Cause- Effect analysis
- The completed diagram also looks like the skeleton of a Fish. Hence the name Fishbone analysis

- Example- let's consider the same incident of application unavailability due to database issue, discussed above as part of '5-why' analysis. A sample Fishbone for this issue may look like the one shown below

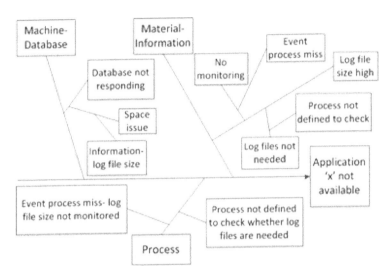

- Thus we arrive at the same root cause as in the case of '5-why' analysis which is to establish a process to check whether log file retention is needed or not and also a process for monitoring the log file size and alerting

Fault tree analysis

- This technique can be used proactively for risk identification and reactively for root cause analysis
- Just like Fishbone analysis, even in this technique, causes and effects are connected to each other and the causes are traced backwards from the effect starting with the problem or issue being investigated
- This technique starts with the problem or issue for which cause is being investigated, stated on top as the starting point of a fault tree
- Then as we saw in Fishbone, high level causes for the problem or issue are identified and documented in boxes connected to the problem with relevant 'and', 'or' gates as relevant
- For each of these high level causes, the question 'why' is asked to identify second level causes which are again captured as boxes connected to the respective high level causes
- The iteration goes on until one is convinced that the root cause has been identified

- Example- Consider the incident of application unavailability due to database issue discussed in both '5-why' and 'Fishbone' analysis techniques above. A Fault Tree analysis for this may look as shown below

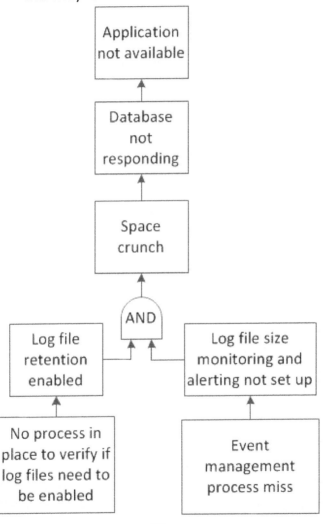

- Thus we arrive at the same root cause as in the case of '5-why' and Fishbone analysis which is to establish a process to check whether log file retention is needed or not and also a process for monitoring the log file size and alerting

Root cause analysis (RCA) Template

Now that the RCA techniques are understood, it is equally important to clearly articulate and present the root cause to customer stakeholders to give them confidence that the problem has been or will be fixed and that the business will not be plagued by disruptions caused by IT incidents. Many a time, this critical link causes dissatisfaction among customers as it is unclear to the customer if the IT support team has identified the root cause and also unclear are the remedial actions planned or implemented to prevent recurring incidents. An RCA template can greatly help clearly present the root cause to customer and also standardize the same across technology teams.

Having worked with many customers, I had the privilege to learn from several RCA templates. Instead of sharing an RCA template, I shall feed your imagination with the below inputs (critical elements of an RCA template) and let it design a template that suits your organizational needs.

Elements of an RCA template:

- problem details
- Root Cause
- corrective and preventive actions

Let's discuss the elements of an RCA template, in detail:

- **Problem details**- The very first section of the RCA template should provide problem impact details which should include the following
  - Problem record number and date it was created
  - Description of the problem including symptoms observed like lack of connectivity
  - Details of all the related incidents (incident number, brief description, incident date)
  - Impact of the problem i.e., actual impact of all the related incidents. It may be quantified through any of the aspects below-
    - Revenue loss ($) if available
    - Number of business hours lost

- Regulatory, statutory, legal or compliance impact
- Physical security (loss of life or property)
- Information security impact (data loss, unauthorized access to data, data integrity issue like data manipulation, etc.,)
- Number of users impacted
- Number of locations impacted

  o In the absence of related incidents i.e., proactive problem identified by the team even before any incident occurrence, impact could be potential instead of actual

- **Root Cause**- This section should contain the root cause. It is important to explain the logical connection between the problem, the high level causes and the root cause. With regards to the root cause section, the template should not be only a documenting form but a guiding force and hence it is important to weave into the RCA template simple yet powerful RCA techniques like '5-why' analysis and Fishbone analysis. Below could serve as a sample

Cause Level	Cause Type	Cause Sub-Type	Cause details
Why1?			
Why2?			
Why3?			
Why4?			
Why5?			

- o In the above sample template if you are able to provide a list of values to choose from in the columns labeled "Cause Type" and "Cause Sub- type", it will guide/ serve the technical teams well to think through probable causes like in a Fishbone analysis
- o You may use the same six areas- 5M and 1E- discussed above in the Fishbone analysis technique as values to choose from under "Cause Type" field
- o Based on consultations with the technology SMEs and your technical experience, you may build a list of commonly observed sub causes to be used as values under "Cause sub-type" field

- Example-
  - You may provide 'Methods (process)' as a value to choose from under "Cause Type" and then provide values like- not defined, not documented, not updated, poor awareness, lack of training, no process controls, lack of review and governance- as values to choose from under the "Cause Sub-type"
  - Consider the example of application unavailability discussed as part for all the RCA techniques above. A sample populated template for the issue may be as shown below

Cause Level	Cause Type	Cause Sub-Type	Cause details
Why1?	Machine (Technology/ Product)	Database failure	Database was not responding due to which application was not available
Why2?	Machine (Technology/ Product)	Database failure	There was a space crunch due to which databse was not responding
Why3?	Material (information)	Information growth	Space crunch on the databse was caused by log file which had grown high (high file size)
Why4?	Method (Process)	Method (Process)	Process not defined to identify which databses need log file enabled and which databases do not
Why4? (Continued)	Method (Process)	Method (Process)	Event management process not operatonal in this case due to which the dabase was not monitoried for log file size and hence there were no alerts calling for remedial actions

- **Corrective and preventive actions**- This section is just as important as the root cause section of the RCA template. Customers are usually keen on knowing not just the cause but the actions planned or implemented to prevent incidents in future
  - This section should include both the corrective actions and also the preventive actions along with action owner, status, planned start date & end date, actual start date & end date for each of the action items
  - As explained in the 'Key Terms' sections of chapter 2 of this book, 'corrective actions' refers to those actions which will prevent recurrence of an incident on the same IT component due to the same cause. This means corrective actions include both the actions that permanently fix the cause on the affected IT component and also those actions which are preventive in nature and prevent recurrence of an incident on the same IT component due to the same cause
  - As explained in the 'Key Terms' sections of chapter 2 of this book, 'preventive actions' refer to actions that shall prevent

recurrence of an incident due to the same root cause on all other IT components in the entire organization that are similar to the affected IT component where corrective actions have been applied

- Example- Consider the application unavailability incident discussed in all the RCA techniques above, for this incident, corrective actions include
  - Clearing the log files on the affected database to resolve the incident
  - Check if storing the log files is required on the affected database? If no (not required), disable the same
  - If yes (required) then on the affected database, set up a monitoring alert to be triggered when the free space is less than a specific threshold say 30%. Also configure automatic execution of a script to clear the log files whenever this alert is triggered
  - All these actions called 'corrective actions' will solve the problem permanently on the affected database but not in the entire IT estate

- Example- in the same example above, preventive actions include
  - Performing checks to determine the need to store log files on all other databases in the organization and where relevant, disable logging
  - Where log files are needed, on all such databases, set up a monitoring alert to be triggered when the free space is less than a specific threshold say 30% or when the log file size exceeds a certain threshold (X GB). Also configure automatic execution of a script to clear the log files whenever such an alert is triggered
  - All these actions called 'preventive actions' will solve the problem permanently in the organization i.e., fix the identified cause on all the databases of the organization

Besides the RCA techniques training for the technical teams and providing the RCA template, it is important to review the RCA internally before publishing the RCA to customers. The review must at the least cover language used (formal and jargon free), articulation and information adequacy and accuracy.

Now that the root cause analysis techniques and articulation are clear, it is time to focus on fixing the root cause!

V. Fixing the problem- Resolution and Closure

- Known error, KEDB

As discussed in 'overview of the problem process' section of chapter 2, the next key steps after root cause identification are identifying workaround, KEDB update and implementing permanent solution. In the previous chapter we discussed RCA techniques to identify the root cause, we now move onto the next steps.

Workaround

Workaround is a solution that resolves an incident temporarily. It is usually quickly implementable in nature so as to decrease the impact of incident through faster resolution.

Known error

A problem is called a known error when root cause and/ or workaround are available

- I have intentionally used 'or' in the above statement because even when the root cause is not known but only a workaround, it is still beneficial to call a 'problem' as 'known error' and publish it to the relevant IT support teams along with the workaround details so that when they come across an incident caused by this known error, they are able to use the published workaround and resolve the incident
- Known errors are important because they are referred to, to get the workaround for faster incident resolution
- When a known error is identified it must be communicated to all relevant IT staff who may need to be aware and use the workaround for faster incident resolution, where relevant, some known errors may have to be communicated to the users as well
  - Example: When a simple action by the user can resolve the incident related to a

known error, the same may be communicated to users as self help

- To ensure that all IT staff have access to the workarounds, known errors are centrally maintained in a database called known error database (KEDB) discussed below
- It is important to track the usage and status of the known errors and the same may be tracked within the KEDB as discussed below

- **Known error sources include**
  - Diagnosis and resolution efforts of technical resources involved in incident management activities. In such cases when the problem record is created, details of the workaround already identified during incident resolution must be captured in the KEDB
  - Workaround may be identified during problem management at which point the problem must be declared a known error and the workaround captured in the KEDB. Sometimes the workaround identified by problem management may be in addition to the workaround already identified during incident management. In such cases the known error will have multiple workarounds and the technical teams involved in incident management may choose to use the most appropriate or most effective of the available workarounds or the best workaround to be used may be decided by the technology SMEs
  - Defects being transitioned into Production along with the workarounds must be

captured as known errors in the KEDB. Problem manager should engage the Development, Testing and deployment teams to gather such information, as such defects are usually identified during Testing

o Similarly defects identified by principal vendors of a product or technology like Aspect, Cisco, Microsoft etc., must be captured along with the workarounds as known errors in the KEDB

Known error Database (KEDB)

This is a repository that holds information about all the known errors along with the associated symptoms, root cause, workaround and status of the known error. Also the related problem record number and status of the problem must be captured. This is one of the most important outputs of the problem process

- This may be maintained in an Excel sheet or in a tool
- This database is different from Knowledge Base which is maintained as a repository of

knowledge artefacts including architecture diagrams, preventive maintenance procedures, troubleshooting steps including diagnosis steps etc.,

- Problem manager must ensure that all the technology teams involved in incident management activities are provided at least read access to the KEDB
- Problem manager must ensure that the incident management staff are trained on how to use or search the KEDB to identify the workaround for faster incident resolution
- Problem manager must ensure that the KEDB is not modified without his/ her review and approval as it is important to maintain the integrity of the KEDB
- Problem manager must maintain the KEDB up-to-date i.e., the problem manager must review any new known errors identified and any updates proposed to the existing known errors and approve updates to the KEDB
- Problem manager must regularly communicate about the KEDB to incident management staff such communication should at least include-
  - Recent updates made to the KEDB

- o Guidance around KEDB access and usage
- o Guidance around providing feedback or proposing updates or changes to the known errors or KEDB
- It is important to track the usage of known errors i.e., every time a known error is used to resolve an incident, it must be recorded. This is useful in two ways
  - o Firstly, it's a metric that demonstrates the effectiveness of the KEDB and the problem process
  - o Secondly, it also allows one to revisit the priority of unresolved problems related to the known errors used for incident resolution so that there is adequate focus and urgency towards resolution of such problems whose impact is constantly increasing as evident from frequent use of the known errors related to such problems
- It is important to track the status of the known error and the related problem record in the KEDB
  - o When a problem record is closed without a permanent resolution then the known error status remains 'open' or 'unresolved' in the KEDB

- When a problem record is closed successfully i.e., after implementation of permanent solution and resolution of the problem then the known error status in the KEDB is marked as 'closed' or 'resolved'
- When a known error with 'resolved' or 'closed' status in the KEDB is used to fix an incident, this must immediately trigger a dialog with the problem manager who must establish the need to resume problem investigation which may even include reopening the problem record
- The common or usual points of failure in the problem process are lack of usage of known errors and where they are used, lack of measurement of their usage. This can be managed or addressed through
  - Sustained education of IT staff on KEDB/ known error usage as part of induction training, periodic refresher trainings and monthly awareness mailers
  - Also through implementing measurement systems to capture and report on known error usage. The measurement system may be tool driven or a manual track of

usage count of each known error in an Excel spreadsheet

Now, let's look at workaround and permanent solution of the problem

Workaround

Workaround is an important output from the problem process used by the incident management staff for faster resolution of incidents.

As discussed in the 'key terms' section of chapter 2, workaround is a solution that resolves an incident temporarily. It is usually quickly implementable in nature so as to decrease the impact of incident through faster resolution. Example:

- A workaround may be- when user of application 'A' complains of error xx1, please unregister the user and re-register the user as an authorized user of the application 'A'. This should resolve the user's incident
- A workaround may be- when a user complains of screen freeze or no response issue with application 'B' while performing a transaction of type 'Trans-x' in the application, manually terminate the specific transaction from the database end. This should resolve the user's incident

- A workaround may be diverting traffic of location 1 to domain controller of location 2 temporarily when there is an issue with domain controller of location 1, to contain business impact at location 1
- An extreme example of a workaround used in a real life situation that I encountered was-there was a network unavailability issue. SMEs identified that the location Firewall was experiencing abnormally high utilization, acting as a bottleneck and causing network unavailability for an entire location affecting thousands of users from several business functions. As no other resolution efforts worked, senior management of business and IT together with the information security leaders decided to bypass the Firewall temporarily to allow business to resume normal operation and continue to engage SMEs to identify and fix the root cause or at least come up with a safer workaround
- Another example of a workaround was a memory leak issue caused an application code. The Application support team realized that it will take a few days to a few weeks to develop and implement a code fix. As a

workaround to prevent incidents due to this problem, the team initiated some daily health checks and housekeeping activities specifically targeting this leak issue while working in parallel on a permanent solution.

Though usually workaround is an activity that resolves an incident, as seen above, sometimes a workaround may focus on some preventive actions that will prevent an incident from occurring while a permanent solution is still being identified and implemented.

Communicate workaround- It is important to ensure that every workaround is communicated to incident management staff and this is achieved by declaring a problem as a known error when a workaround is available, adding the known error to the KEDB and communicating KEDB updates to teams involved in incident management as discussed above.

Implement workaround- It is important to adhere to the organization's change management process while implementing a workaround. Besides the change process and the approvals obtained there in, sometimes there may be a specific customer stakeholder identified to approve a workaround as 'acceptable' in which case such a stakeholder's approval has to be sought first and only then the workaround must be implemented following the change process. The related problem record must be linked to the change record raised to implement the workaround. This may be done in the ticketing tool or by including the details of the change record number in the problem record.

Permanent solution

Besides workaround, it is important that a permanent solution is identified and implemented to fix the problem or the root cause permanently and prevent incident recurrence which is the ultimate purpose of the problem management process.

CAPA- Permanent solution includes corrective actions and preventive actions (CAPA). Corrective actions are those which permanently solve the problem on an affected configuration item (CI) whereas preventive actions are those that solve the problem permanently in all other similar CIs in the entire organization. Ideally, corrective and preventive actions must be shared with the customer when sharing the root cause. Please refer to 'Root Cause Analysis (RCA) template' topic of the section named- 'How to'- RCA techniques and RCA template- of chapter 4 of this book for detailed explanation on CAPA with examples.

Implement the permanent solution- It is important to adhere to the organization's change management process while implementing the permanent solution. Besides the change process and the approvals obtained there in, sometimes there may be a specific customer stakeholder identified to approve a permanent solution as 'acceptable' in which case such a stakeholder's approval has to be sought first and only then the permanent solution must be implemented following the change process. The related problem record must be linked to the change record raised to implement the permanent solution. This may be done in the ticketing tool or by including the details of the change record number in the problem record.

Regular tracking

It is important that the problem manager tracks the entire lifecycle of the problem right from its identification. problem manager must ensure that a problem record is created for every potential problem that needs investigation as discussed in chapter 3 ('Identifying the problem') of this book. Thereafter, the problem manager must track the progress of the problem investigation, implementation of workaround, identification of permanent solution and implementation of permanent solution through regular meetings held weekly or once in two weeks with the problem owners and technology SMEs to gather updates and to ensure that the same is captured in the problem records.

Monitor

After implementing a permanent solution, it is important to verify the effectiveness of the solution implemented.

- This is done by monitoring the problem for a certain period of time agreed between stakeholders like technology SMEs, problem owner and customer stakeholders
- This monitoring period may extend from days to weeks to even months depending on nature of the problem
- Example- If a permanent solution is implemented to resolve a problem experienced by the Finance team during end of month or quarter period, the monitoring period may have to extend up to the end of month or quarter for verification or confirmation of resolution
- During the monitoring period if incidents occur due to the same cause then the problem owner and the technology teams will revisit the problem investigation and identify

the correct root cause and/ or permanent solution as relevant

Monitoring is important to confirm or verify problem resolution i.e., effectiveness of the permanent solution implemented and then the next step will be problem closure.

Close- problem closure

This is the final step in the problem life cycle. There can be various scenarios leading to problem closure and they are:

- **Successful problem resolution-** Continuing from the previous section when a permanent solution is implemented and no incidents are observed during the monitoring period, the problem record may be closed as successful. Also, status of the problem record and the related known error must be updated in the KEDB as 'closed'
- **Root cause not identified-** Sometimes, technology teams may not be in a position to identify the root cause
  - o This may be because of lack of technical information from incident management or

inability to recreate incidents observed due to the problem or inability to identify the root cause due to any other reason even by the principal Vendor of the Product or technology

- In such cases, the problem record must be closed indicating that root cause has been inconclusive and the related known error in the KEDB must remain in 'open' status along with the correct status of the related problem
- Example- I have seen many cases where root cause is not identified due to lack of device logs and also inability to recreate the same incident again in non-production environment. One such case was a server reboot performed to resolve an incident, without capturing the server logs before the reboot

- **Root cause identified but not permanent solution**- Just like the above scenario, sometimes, root cause may be known but permanent solution may not be available even after engaging the principal Vendor of the Product or technology. This may be due to Product bugs or technical limitations etc.,

- In such cases, the problem record must closed indicating that the permanent solution is not available and the related known error in the KEDB must remain in 'open' status along with the correct status of the related problem
- Usually in such cases the principal vendor may provide a workaround (Ex: periodic reboot or applying a hotfix) to be used for incident resolution or prevention
- Permanent solution identified but not implemented- In some scenarios, a permanent solution may be identified but may not be acceptable to customer stakeholder for implementation due to cost or technology or other business considerations
  - In such cases it is important to capture the problem as a risk in the Risk Register database along with the customer's risk response strategy. The risk details like risk ID and risk response must be captured in the problem record and then the problem record must be closed indicating that the permanent solution is not implemented

- The related known error in the KEDB must remain in 'open' status along with the correct status of the related problem

In all the above scenarios, before problem closure the problem manager must ensure that the problem record contains all the relevant information gathered or used during the problem cycle like related incident details, root cause investigation details including device logs etc., where available root cause and workaround identified, related known error ID/ number, details of the permanent solution implemented if any, observations from the monitoring period post implementation of the permanent solution, details of related change requests raised to implement the workaround or the permanent solution, details of the risk and customer's response in case permanent solution is not implemented.

VI.   The business Impact

- Reporting

Besides problem identification and resolution to prevent incidents, it is also important to communicate the benefits of the problem management process to all stakeholders most importantly the customer or business. Problem manager must hold weekly or at least monthly reviews with the customer stakeholders to communicate the business benefits from the problem process implementation or process activities. The problem manager must publish weekly and monthly performance reports to be reviewed during these meetings.

I have learnt over the years implementing problem management process that the most effective demonstration of benefits of the problem process is the 'before/ after' report. Apart from the metrics that are commonly reported (that are listed below), the game- changer in the report will be inclusion of a 'before/ after' representation of incident reduction for each problem resolved during the reporting period. The 'before/ after' representation in the report may be in the form of a graph as shown below.

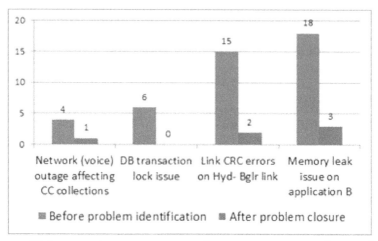

This graph represents the average number of incidents per month for each issue, before problem identification and after the problem closure. Network voice, data link and memory leak issues mentioned above are those where the related problem may have been closed without implementing permanent solution but with only preventive workarounds being implemented.

Similar graphical representations can be included separately for proactively identified problems and reactive problems as well in the weekly/ monthly problem performance reports.

Key Performance Indicators (KPI) –

Besides the 'before/ after' incident reduction, other Key Performance Indicators that may be included in the problem management performance reports are listed below (not an exhaustive list):

- Number of problems raised and number of problems resolved
- Number of incidents prevented by resolved problems
- Number of problems identified proactively
- Number of known errors identified (and published into the KEDB)
- Number of known errors used for incident resolution or Percentage incidents resolved using known errors
- Percentage or number of RCAs published per agreed timelines

Tips for effective reporting:

- Publish only what conveys process effectiveness
- Publish to the right stakeholders (include the one's needed and exclude the one's not needed)
- Publish the report consistently per agreed timelines

VII.   The Hero!

- Problem manager- Skills, Role & Responsibilities

As discussed in the very first chapter, over and above the heroics of incident resolution, what the IT support team also needs is the heroics of problem management i.e., to proactively or at least reactively identify problems, identify and fix root cause and there by prevent incidents. The person who drives the entire IT support team towards such heroics is the problem manager.

Problem manager is the Hero working like a Movie Director behind the scenes to ensure a healthy IT estate, to minimize incident occurrence or at least recurrence. This is certainly not a loved role as sometimes it may involve a lot of questioning/ grilling / probing technology teams especially while publishing the root cause and also pushing all the IT support teams to proactively identify problems in the IT estate.

Role and Responsibilities

The role and responsibilities of a problem manager are listed below. These may not be exhaustive but are the ones observed over the years on the ground in many organizations:

- Implement problem management process i.e., ensure that all the process activities are carried out by relevant stakeholders
- Educate IT support teams and other relevant stakeholders on the problem process through training sessions and awareness mailers
- Drive proactive problem identification i.e., drive IT support teams and other relevant stakeholders to perform activities like data analysis etc., to identify problems proactively
- Ensure reactive problem identification is in place
- Ensure all problems are recorded and investigated
- Monitor progress of problem investigation at least through weekly meetings
- Review and publish root cause to customer and other stakeholders

- Ensure known errors along with their workarounds are recorded in the known error database (KEDB)
- Maintain an up-to-date and accurate KEDB
- Maintain data integrity of the KEDB
- Promote/ drive KEDB usage
- Monitor implementation of permanent resolution
- Facilitate discussions needed to identify root cause, workaround and permanent resolution
- Verify problem resolution
- Ensure adequate and accurate documentation in problem records
- Publish regular process performance reports
- Conduct periodic process performance reviews with customer and other stakeholders
- Drive continual improvement activities for the problem process
- Liaise with the problem process owner to effect problem process design changes needed
- Liaise with technology teams to automate relevant process activities

- Ensure availability of all data needed for proactive problem identification
- Secure sponsorship including people resources required for implementing the problem process
- Encourage and drive any or all other activities per organizational needs for preventing incidents

Skills, knowledge and experience

The key skills needed to effectively drive the problem process and carry out the above listed responsibilities are:

- Eye for detail and ability to analyze high volume of data to identify trends, patterns etc.,
- Ability to identify the right data needed for analysis
- Patience to persist, given the long time some problems may need for investigation
- Probing skills to probe the technology teams as needed during problem investigation
- Ability to quickly comprehend unfamiliar subjects and/ or technical information

- Knowledge of popular root cause analysis techniques
- Ability to train and guide technology teams in usage of root cause analysis techniques
- Ability to drive people and teams (to carry out problem process activities and adhere to the problem process)
- Excellent Communication skills
- Ability to prepare insightful reports
- Ability to build and maintain healthy business/ professional relationship with customer and all other stakeholders of the problem process
- Ability to facilitate discussions when needed, among various stakeholders including customer, Principal vendors, technology teams and other service providers
- Level 2 or at least level 1 engineer knowledge in at least one technology will be an advantage
- Knowledge of IT service management tools or ticketing tools will be an advantage
- Experience of about 3- 5 years in IT service management/ support operations is desired

VIII. Implementing the problem process

- Pre- Requisites (Eight keys)

The following eight key Pre- requisites are required to implement the problem management process effectively. The first four on this list were also discussed as part of problem identification in chapter 2:

- **CTI**: Categorization scheme (CTI) used for incidents must be well understood and must be consistently followed across all technology teams and the service Desk operators
  - ○ Example- An outlook incident (unable to send/ receive mails) reported by a user must be recorded using the same category, type and item (CTI) fields in the ticketing tool, irrespective of who records the incident from the Service Desk or technology teams or even if logged by the user himself or herself though a self- help portal

- **CI mapping**- Every incident at least the higher priority incidents being mapped to a Configuration Item (CI) can significantly increase the effectiveness of proactive problem identification activity because specific CIs with repeat incidents (which indicates potential problem) can be identified if the CI mapping exists
- **Resolution code**- This is an important field in the incident form which, if designed with the right set of values to choose from and if populated diligently by resources resolving incidents, will be a potent source of data for proactive problem identification
- **Data availability**- Another pre- requisite which was a real challenge in some of the problem management engagements was non-availability of monitoring data required for data analysis for proactive problem identification. Problem manager needs to work with the monitoring tools team to get this in place and get management buy in as needed
- **Means to build a KEDB**- There must be some way/ means to build a KEDB and provide known error and workaround information to

technology teams involved in incident management. It could be either a tool or at least an Excel spreadsheet that can be made accessible to all resources involved in incident resolution

- **Means to measure known error usage**- There must be a measurement method put in place to capture usage of known errors. This is important to identify problems that need re-investigation and also to demonstrate the effectiveness of the problem management process

- The problem manager engaged to drive the process must possess the skills listed in the previous chapter 7 (The Hero!). Some of the key skills that he/ she must possess are ability to build strong business or professional relationship with all stakeholders especially the technology teams, possess knowledge of RCA techniques, have good probing skills, ability to drive people/ teams and perseverance

- **Management support**- Last but most certainly not the least, management Support. Top down approach is critical to the success of this process

As already highlighted as part of skills required for a problem manager in chapter 7 (The Hero!) and also in the above section, it is important for the problem manager to build healthy professional relationship with technology teams to drive the problem management process because driving this process involves interactions and working with many teams across the IT service provider organization, customer organization and even vendors.

Besides building relationship, the following tips were hard learnt in my experience of implementing the problem management process. A problem manager may use these tips to drive the problem process:

- **Understand the as-is**
  - Understand the existing set of problem management activities carried out by the teams either as part of problem management process or generally as part of IT service operations
  - Identify the key internal (Example- technology SMEs) and customer

stakeholders (Example- Customer's IT service management owner or customer's 'partner performance manager') for the problem process

- o Review the existing process documents if any like the KEDB, problem management process document, problem process performance reports, templates like RCA template etc.,
- o Review the categorization scheme (CTI) used for categorizing incidents and problems

- **Customer pain points**
  - o Engage with the key customer stakeholders for the problem process and understand their pain points related to the problem process like poor RCA quality, lack of proactive measures to prevent incidents etc.,
  - o Also gather internal customer pain points related to problem management activities by engaging the Delivery manager, service Desk staff, technology SMEs, Level1/ Level 2 engineers from technology teams who get engaged in the incident management process for incident resolution

- **Plan**
  - List out activities needed to improve the problem management as per the best practices and also the activities needed to address the specific pain points of the stakeholders gathered above
  - Review if any design changes are needed to the problem management process and ensure that the required changes are made
- **Common actions**- Some common actions that I have implemented across several engagements successfully and which you may draw from and implement as appropriate to your organization are:
  - Make it mandatory for every major incident and high priority incident to be mapped to a problem ticket. Please note that this does not mean creation of a new problem record for each such incident but making sure that every such incident is either mapped to an existing problem record or to a new problem record as relevant

- Whenever there is a need to identify root cause of an incident, there must be a problem record
- Ensure categorization scheme (CTI) used is same for problems and incidents
- Ensure categorization scheme (CTI) used for incidents is cleaned up as needed and all the incident management teams including the Service Desk are trained and possess a common understanding on usage of CTI. Ensure any inconsistencies in CTI are regularly identified through ticket audits and addressed
- Identify data needed for proactive problem identification like monitoring data, incident data etc., Also identify data which already have reliable data sources in place and the one's which do not
- Engage relevant teams like tools teams, technology teams etc., and start gathering data needed for analysis or at least ensure such a data source is built to provide data when needed, for analysis
- Build a virtual team – Seek a single point of contact (SPOC) for problem management process from each of the

technology teams. Train these SPOCs on the problem process in general, the problem process followed in the organization, data analysis techniques and RCA techniques. Assign specific set of problem process activities to these SPOCs like monthly data analysis of their team's incident and monitoring data, tracking the progress of every problem assigned to their team etc.,

o Data analysis- Ensure data analysis is performed at least once a month to proactively identify problems. This SPOCs mentioned above can be coached on data analysis aspect over a period of time

o Weekly meetings- Conduct weekly internal problem management meetings with technology teams to track the progress of every problem record and ensure that the problem record is updated

o RCA training- Ensure RCA techniques training for all technology SMEs and technical resources who may be involved with root cause analysis activity of the problem process. This training must at a minimum cover '5-why' analysis,

'Fishbone' analysis and 'Fault tree analysis' discussed in chapter 4 (what's causing it?) of this book as these are most widely used RCA techniques for identifying root cause of a problem

○ RCA template- Where required, develop an RCA template with all the essential elements as discussed in chapter 4 (what's causing it?) of this book. This can help better articulate the root cause

○ 100% RCA review- Ensure that every RCA is reviewed by the relevant technology SME to assure technical adequacy and accuracy. Also, where required another review either by the problem manager or any other stakeholder to verify the articulation, information adequacy and accuracy, use of jargon free language and a logical connection between the problem and the root cause

○ Build KEDB- Ensure that a KEDB is put in place at least in an Excel spread sheet and the same is accessible to all technical teams and other teams involved in resolving incidents. Ensure 'write' privileges for the KEDB is restricted to maintain the KEDB data integrity

- o KEDB usage- Train all resources involved in incident management including the service Desk staff on KEDB usage
- o Verify resolution- For every problem where a permanent solution is implemented, ensure that a monitoring period is agreed and the problem is monitored during that period to check if the problem is resolved or if there any incidents observed due to the same cause/ problem
- o 'Before/ after' report- Ensure at least monthly problem process performance report is shared with all stakeholders, especially the customer stakeholders. Also, ensure that the report includes 'before/ after' data as explained in chapter 6 (The business Impact) of this book
- **Prioritize and implement**- Implement those actions first which can yield quick results or benefits (low hanging fruits) and win customer confidence and then follow it up with the actions that may take time, that may

be difficult to drive but yield long term, sustained and significant business benefits

- **Solicit feedback**- Build a forum to seek feedback from all stakeholders especially customer stakeholders about the problem process and their satisfaction levels and areas of dissatisfaction with the problem management process. This may be an automated survey or a discussion/ agenda item of problem process review meetings

- **Monthly customer review**- At least once a month, conduct a problem process performance review with the customer and all other stakeholders to discuss the benefits or effectiveness of the problem process and areas of improvement if any

- **Continual Improvement**- Ensure a continual improvement culture. Regularly identify areas of improvement for the problem process and drive the identified improvements to improve problem process effectiveness. Report such continual improvement initiatives as well in the problem process performance reports

These are tips from my experience and are certainly not exhaustive!

The commonly performed activities of a problem manager may be segregated into the following daily, weekly and monthly activities:

Daily activities

- Review last 24 hours IT operations reports to gather information about any major incidents, high priority incidents, failed changes and any other service performance or availability issues
- Discuss such issues identified with technology teams
- Ensure problem record is created for every major incident, high priority incident and other deserving issues
- Review RCA status reports and follow up on pending RCA
- Publish daily RCA status report
- Engage technology teams, where needed facilitate problem investigation discussions between technology teams and other stakeholders to identify the root cause, workaround and permanent solution

- Review RCAs ready to be published to customer
- Follow up on the progress of 'open' problems marked for review and mark the 'next review date' for each of them
- Review information and/ or feedback provided by all the stakeholders including the Service Desk, the technology teams involved in incident management, customer stakeholder, users etc., and identify the need to create any problem record
- Follow up on corrective and preventive actions if any, scheduled for implementation on that day

Weekly activities

- Publish weekly problem management process performance reports
- Conduct an internal problem review meeting with all the internal stakeholders to get an update on the problem status and the problem investigation and resolution efforts. Ensure that the same is captured in the respective problem records
- Follow up with problem management SPOCs (virtual team) from all the technology teams and check if any potential problems have been identified
- Conduct a problem review meeting with the customer stakeholder to go over the problem management activities especially the activities around all the unresolved problems

Monthly activities

- Publish monthly problem management process performance reports
- Conduct a problem review meeting with the customer stakeholder to go over the 'before/after' report, problem process KPIs and other problem management activities especially the activities around all the unresolved problems
- Follow up with the (virtual team) problem management SPOCs of every technology team to seek results of monthly data analysis and the proactive problems identified thereby
- Attend customer meetings focused on performance of IT services, to identify potential problems. Such meetings may be specific to technology teams or general/ common delivery performance review, the problem manager must attend such meetings

IX. I am a Hero!

- Self- Certify through Scenario based exam for a problem manager

Equipped with theoretical knowledge of the problem process and practical guidance on process implementation, it's time for a knowledge check. Put your knowledge and skills to test through the below check before jumping into the sea of life of a problem manager- *May this be your paddling pool!* All the Best!

Instructions:

- There are 20 questions −6 theory questions and 14 practical, scenario- based questions
- Answer all the questions
- Each question offers four options to choose from, with only one option being the correct answer
- Each question carries one mark
- Correct answer gives you one mark and wrong answer gives zero, no negative marking
- Pass score is 70% (14 marks)
- Time available- 20 minutes

Theory questions

1. Which of the following describes incident and problem
   a) Incident is an interruption to IT service. Problem is the permanent solution to every incident
   b) Incident needs a change to an IT component. Problem is an underlying cause of incident
   c) Incident is an interruption to IT service. Problem is an underlying cause of incidents
   d) Incident is an underlying cause of problems. Problem is an interruption to IT service

Your response: _____

2. Which of the following best describes incident and problem management processes?
   a) Incident management is Fire Fighting. Problem management is root cause of the Fire
   b) Incident management is root cause of the Fire. Problem management is Fire Prevention
   c) Incident management is Fire Fighting. Problem management is the Fire wood
   d) Incident management is Fire Fighting. problem management is Fire Prevention

Your response: _____

3. Which of the following is the set of root cause analysis techniques discussed in this book?
   a) Fishbone, 5-Why, FMEA
   b) Fishbone, Fault Tree analysis and '5-why' analysis
   c) Fishbone, FMEA, Fault Tree analysis
   d) Fault Tree analysis, '5-why' analysis and FMEA

Your response: _____

4. What is a known error and where is it stored?
   a) Known error is an incident that has occurred before and hence is known to IT staff. They are stored in an Excel spreadsheet
   b) Known error is a problem record that has more than 3 related incidents. They are stored in problem database
   c) A problem is called a known error when root cause and/ or workaround are available. Known errors are stored in the KEDB
   d) A problem is called a known error when root cause and/ or workaround are available. They are stored in problem database

Your response: _____

5. Which of the following describes corrective Actions and preventive Actions (CAPA) as discussed in this book?

a) Corrective actions prevent recurrence of an incident on the same CI due to the same cause. Preventive actions prevent recurrence of the same incident due to the same cause on all other similar CIs in the organization

b) Corrective actions prevent recurrence of an incident on the same CI due to the same cause. Preventive actions are those actions taken to resolve incidents during incident management

c) Corrective actions are those actions taken to resolve incidents during incident management. Preventive actions prevent recurrence of the same incident due to the same cause on all other similar CIs in the organization

d) Preventive actions prevent recurrence of an incident on the same CI due to the same cause. Corrective actions prevent recurrence of the same incident due to the same cause on all other similar CIs in the organization

Your response: _____

6. Which of the following is/ are outputs of the problem process?
   a) Root Cause and workaround
   b) Permanent solution
   c) Request for change
   d) All of the above

Your response: _____

Practical questions:

Scenario: RCA performed for a major incident identified a missing patch provided by the vendor as the cause.

7. What are the preventive actions you would advocate as the problem manager?
   a) Apply the patch on all similar configuration items to prevent a similar incident due to the same cause on those CIs
   b) Define a process to identify the need for patching for this specific type of CI
   c) Define a process to identify the need for patching for every relevant technology
   d) All of the above

Your response: _____

Scenario: As a problem manager, during data analysis you notice repeat incidents triggered by monitoring alerts.

8. What should your next steps be?
   a) Ignore such incidents as they are not incidents reported by users
   b) Engage the respective technology teams and raise problem record for issues that need further investigation
   c) Share the data with the technology leads and leave it at that
   d) None of the above

Your response: _____

Scenario: As a problem manager, during monitoring data analysis you notice frequent spikes in CPU utilization of a set of servers. None of them have breached the critical threshold and have not caused any business impact.

9. What should your next steps be?
    a) Ignore the incidents as there is no business impact
    b) Recommend an immediate capacity expansion (addition of processors)
    c) Engage the respective technology teams and raise problem record for issues that need further investigation
    d) None of the above

Your response: _____

Scenario: As a problem manager, during incident data analysis you notice inconsistent use of categorization scheme (CTI).

10. What should your next steps be to improve CTI usage?
    a) Ignore the issue as CTI usage is related to incident management, not problem management
    b) Engage the incident management team and drive CTI usage improvement initiatives because consistent usage of CTI is a pre-requisite for proactive problem identification
    c) Share the information with the incident management team and leave it at that
    d) None of the above

Your response: _____

Scenario: As a problem manager, during monitoring data analysis you notice frequent disk space issues in a set of servers. None of them have breached the critical threshold and have not caused any business impact.

11. What should your next steps be?
    a) Ignore the incidents as there is no business impact
    b) Recommend an immediate capacity expansion (addition of disks)
    c) Engage the respective technology teams and raise problem record for issues that need further investigation
    d) None of the above

Your response: _____

Scenario: As a problem manager, during incident data analysis you notice that values available for 'resolution code' field in the incident form are not enabling problem identification.

12. What should your next steps be?
    a) Engage the incident management team and revise values provided for 'resolution code' field in the incident form because it is an important field that aids proactive problem management
    b) Ignore the issue as 'resolution code' field is related to incident management, not problem management
    c) Share the information with the incident management team and leave it at that
    d) None of the above

Your response: _____

Scenario: As a problem manager, during incident data analysis you notice that CIs are not mapped to alert triggered incidents due to tool limitation. Neither is the CI name or ID consistently included in incident description by the Event management team that creates such incidents.

13. What should your next steps be in view of proactive problem identification?
    a) Ignore the issue as it is not related to problem management
    b) Share the information with the Event manager and leave it at that
    c) Engage the event manager and drive improvements to standardize the incident description used by the Event management team when creating incidents for monitoring alerts and also include CI name or ID in the description of such incidents
    d) None of the above

Your response: _____

Scenario: As a problem manager, during monitoring data analysis you notice that the tool is unable to provide CI details as separate field for analysis. You also notice that CI name or ID is part of the alert description for all the alerts generated by the tool. However, it is difficult to extract CI details from such description in its current form or state

14. What should your next steps be to?
    a) Ignore the issue as it is not related to problem management
    b) Ignore the issue as this is related to tool limitation and nothing much can be done about text fields/ data used in the description
    c) Share the issue with the event manager and leave it at that
    d) Engage the event manager and drive improvements to standardize the alert description configured in the monitoring tool for each alert type ensuring CI name or ID is so placed that it is easily extractable from the description using Excel spreadsheet functions

Your response: _____

Scenario: As a problem manager, you identify that a problem record is raised for a major incident only if RCA is not known during major incident resolution

15. Is this acceptable? What should your next steps be to?
    a) Yes, no need to raise a problem record when RCA is identified during incident process
    b) Take steps to ensure that every major incident is mapped to a problem record. The RCA must be included in the problem record and also corrective and preventive actions must be tracked to closure as part of problem process
    c) Ignore the issue as the technology teams may not be interested in creating problem tickets when they already know the root cause
    d) Engage the major incident team to ensure that they create a problem record for every major incident. Attach the RCA when it is already identified as part of major incident resolution and immediately close such problem tickets dropping a mail to the problem manager

Your response: _____

Scenario: As a problem manager, you have just joined an IT team and you realize that problem tickets are closed once RCA is published and all stakeholders seems comfortable with the practice

16. Is this acceptable? What should your next steps be to?
    a) This is perfectly ok because the main purpose of the problem process is root cause identification
    b) This is ok because it is best to remain quiet for the first 2 months of joining the IT team as problem manager and not disturb the as-is
    c) Ignore the issue because all stakeholders are comfortable
    d) Engage the relevant stakeholders and explain that as per best practice, the problem record must remain open beyond RCA identification for tracking CAPA to closure and verifying problem resolution

Your response: _____

Scenario: As a problem manager, you have just joined an IT team and you realize that customer is not happy with the RCA quality. You realize that the technical teams find the root cause but the RCA is not well documented and does not establish a clear relation between the problem and the root cause

17. What should your next steps be to?
    a) Ignore it because the root cause is correctly identified it is mere documentation issue
    b) (Re)Design the RCA template used to articulate and publish the root cause to ensure that a clear logical relationship is highlighted between the problem and the root cause. Agree the template with the customer and train the technology teams on its use
    c) Ask the customer to provide an RCA template of his choice because it is the customer who find the articulation an issue
    d) Either b or c

Your response: _____

Scenario: As a problem manager, you have just joined an IT team and you realize that customer is not happy with the RCA quality. You realize that the technical teams provide a superficial or high- level cause and are not trained on any RCA techniques

18. What should your next steps be to?
    a) Train the technology teams on popular RCA techniques. Be part of RCA discussions for the first few months and ensure that all the technology teams understand and effectively use the techniques to be able to identify the root cause moving beyond the superficial or high- level cause. Ensure at least one level of internal SME level review before RCA is published to the customer to ensure that the root cause has been identified
    b) Ignore it because root cause identification is the responsibility of technology teams not the problem manager
    c) Ignore the issue. It is best for a new problem manager not disturb the as-is practices
    d) Ask the customer to provide a solution for the issue identified by the customer

Your response: _____

Scenario: As a problem manager, you have just joined an IT team and you realize that customer is not happy with the RCA quality. You realize that the technical teams provide the right cause but it is poorly documented (language issues- use of Jargon, not logically organized etc.,)

19. What should your next steps be to?
    a) Ignore it because root cause identification is the responsibility of technology teams
    b) Ignore the issue. It is best for a new problem manager not to disturb the as-is practices
    c) Ask the customer to provide a solution for the issue identified by the customer
    d) (Re)Design the RCA template used to ensure that information is logically organized. Identify specific senior engineers from each of the technology teams who would document the RCA using the RCA template. Provide such engineers requisite training on use of language like jargon- free, right grammar etc., Ensure at least one level of internal review to ensure that the right cause has been identified and it is well documented, before publishing the RCA to customer

Your response: _____

Scenario: As a problem manager, you have just joined an IT team and you realize that problem tickets are closed immediately after implementing the permanent solution.

20. Is this acceptable? What should your next steps be to?

   a) It is perfectly ok to close the problem ticket after implementing permanent solution. No action needs to be taken by the problem manager in this case

   b) Ignore the issue because it is best for a new problem manager to remain quiet for the first 2 months and not disturb the as-is practices

   c) Take steps to ensure that every problem, after implementation of permanent solution, is monitored for an agreed period of time to check for problem resolution i.e., to check that incident are not occurring after implementing the permanent solution. Ensure that problem ticket is closed only after this monitoring and verification

   d) (Re)Design the RCA template used to ensure that information is logically organized. Identify specific senior engineers from each of the technology teams who would document the RCA using the RCA template. Provide such engineers requisite training on use of language like jargon- free, right grammar etc., Ensure at least one level of internal review to ensure that the right cause has been identified and it is well documented, before publishing the RCA to customer

Your response: _____

Please refer to Appendix (chapter 10) for answers to the above 20 questions and check your scores.

I am certain you would have passed with flying colours!

X. Appendix

KPI   Key Performance Indictor

OEM   Original Equipment Manufacturer

OLA   Operational Level Agreement

PM   Problem management

RCA   Root Cause Analysis

SLA   Service Level Agreement

SME   Subject Matter Expert

SPOC Single point of contact

Answers to 'self- certify' test of chapter 9

Question number	Correct answer
1	c
2	d
3	b
4	c
5	a
6	d
7	d
8	b
9	c
10	b
11	c
12	a
13	C
14	d
15	b
16	d
17	b
18	a
19	d
20	c

Mind- map for problem process

1. Identify Problem

1. Reactive- From major incidents or high priority or repeat incidents
2. Proactive- Data analysis of incident/ monitoring/ utilization/ performance data. Bugs/ testing defects information from Vendors or deployment teams
3. preventive- Attend change control meetings to review change planning & testing. Start/ stop recovery procedures

2. Record Problem

1. Problem description, impact (applications/ users impact, $ value, compliance/ regulatory issues etc.,)
2. Suspected cause, any workaround or Vendor hotfix, Major incident report and related incidents' details

3. Categorize and Prioritize

1. Categorize (CTI) using the same CTI scheme as incidents and assign to the right technology team
2. Prioritize using impact and urgency matrix so that problems with higher impact or greater urgency are resolved

4. Identify Root cause

1. Use any popular RCA technique like '5-why', 'Fishbone' or 'Fault tree'
2. RCA template- ensure there is a connection between problem and root cause
4. Internal RCA reviews to check that the root cause has been identified and ensure Jargon free language and correct grammar
5. Include CAPA. CA- Fix the cause permanently on the affected CI. PA- Fix the cause permanently on all other similar CIs in the organization

5. Identify and implement workaround

1. workaround- temporarily resolves the incident. Usually something that can be implemented quickly
2. Follow change process as needed to implement the workaround
3. When a workaround is known, call the problem a Known Error (KE) and update the Known Error Database (KEDB)
4. KEDB should have status of Known Error, status of related problem and also number of times KE is used to resolve incidents
5. Workaround may sometimes be preventive in nature i.e., temporary measures to prevent incidents

6. Identify and implement workaround

1. Permanent solution- permanently resolves the cause/ problem,
2. It includes both CA and PA
3. Implementation may take time
4. Follow change process as needed to implement the workaround

7. Monitor and close

Monitor
1. After the permanent solution is implemented, monitor the problem for an agreed period to verify if it is resolved or incidents occurs due to the problem
2. If not resolved, re-investigate as needed

Close
1. If the problem is resolved, close as successful, also mark the KE and problem as closed in the KEDB
2. If RCA not found or permanent solution not found or permanent solution is found but cannot be implemented, close the problem with reason/ sub-status 'unresolved'. Leave the KE open and update problem status in the KEDB.
3. In the above case, raise a Risk and include risk details in the problem ticket
4. All the information related to problem investigation must be in the ticket before closure

A pocket guide for popular RCA techniques

'5-Why' Analysis

1. Ask first 'why'- what caused the incident?

2. Response to the first 'why' must be questioned by another 'why' (second 'why')

3. and so on until one is convinced that the root cause has been identified

4. Response to each 'why' should focus on process or product and not blaming people!

Fish Bone Analysis

1. Provides six areas (5M and 1 E) to think through the probable causes

2. Machine (product), Man (people skills, head count), Material (information), Measurements (reports and review), Methods (processes) and External factors (not in organization control- Ex: strike, natural disasters)

3. For every probable cause under each of these six areas, again apply '5-why' analysis to drill down to the root cause

Fault Tree Analysis

1. State the problem or issue for which cause is being investigated, as the starting point of a fault tree
2. Ask first 'why'- what caused the incident
3. Join these high- level causes to the issue using 'and'/ 'or' logical gates
4. For each of these high-level causes, repeat '5-why' analysis to get to the root cause

Remember that these techniques do not replace a technical resource rather support or guide the technical root cause analysis by providing a structured approach

P

permanent fix, 10
permanent solution, 50
pre- requisites to
   implement PM, 57
preventive actions, 10
preventive problem
   identification, 31
prioritize, 15, 16
proactive problem
   identification, 20
problem, 9
problem closure, 51
problem management, 9
problem management
   report, 53
problem recording, 14

R

RCA techniques, 34
RCA Template, 42
reactive problem
   identification, 30
Record problem, 14
role and responsibilities,
   55
root cause analysis, 32

S

skills, 56

T

temporary fix, 10

W

weekly activities, 61
workaround, 10, 46, 49

Thank you for investing time in this book. I hope it has helped!

Wish you continued success in your journey as a problem manager!

I invite your feedback. Please write to me on topics that you'd like added or elaborated in this book and also any topics that you think might interest readers- siv_santh@yahoo.com

www.ingramcontent.com/pod-product-compliance
Lightning Source LLC
Chambersburg PA
CBHW052141070326
40690CB00047B/1337